To Hermann
A grand American

Jan 5/18/1

REASON, JUSTICE AND COMMON SENSE

A COLLECTION OF ESSAYS FROM THE SIERRA SAGE

Leonard A. Semas

§

Sierra Sage Publishing
Carson City

First Printing

Published by
Sierra Sage Publishing
Carson City, NV

Library of Congress Control Number: 2009908986

ISBN 10: 978-003-764-0
ISBN 13: 978-978-003-764-2

To order additional copies, arrange for interviews
or speaking engagements, please contact us at:
Sierra Sage Publishing
333 W Proctor St.
Carson City, NV 89703
(775) 882-8258
www.sierrasage.com
or
www.reasonjusticeandcommonsense.com

Volume and reseller discounts available

Formatting, Editing, and Cover by: Sierra Sage Publishing

Printed in the United States of America
First printing: October 2009

DEDICATION

To my family and friends, an eclectic collection of people with little in common except good hearts, good heads and good times shared. To my Glen Eagles "family" who argued, inspired, criticized, and critiqued, especially my final draft readers: Doc and Mary, Jim and Sharon, Mary, Diane, Liz, Gary, Brian, Big John, Bill, Ron and Al.

To my teachers in life, some in the education system, some not. Some taught from books, some from example. All required that true learning come from within.

To my son, who I hope will find as much in the wisdom of his father as *his* father did in his. *Experientia docet.*

To the Founders of our nation, who I believe were the smartest collection of men to have ever inhabited the earth and for the blessings of liberty secured by their brilliance and their blood. Without freedom, there is nothing. They knew that. We must never forget.

Leonard A. Semas

But a Constitution of Government once changed from Freedom, can never be restored. Liberty, once lost, is lost forever.
  ~ John Adams

§

Excerpts From
Reason, Justice and Common Sense

"An American birthright is optimism. From the daunting challenge of the fight to secure our first freedoms from England, we have always seen fit to challenge adversity. If the glass is half empty, we'll fill it. If the battle is above our ability, we'll rise to it. If the need is greater than our capacity, we'll meet it. Whether soaring to the unknown risks of heavenly exploration, or facing the inevitable challenges on earth, Americans have the courage, tenacity, and inventiveness to shrink from nothing that limits them."

§

"Wealth is created by private actions. Through the combination of land, labor, capital, management, and creativity, we build, make and grow all that creates wealth. In the process, we create jobs, raise living standards, and empower all to rise to their interests and abilities. Government does not create jobs or wealth; it grows nothing (except debt), it makes nothing (except laws and regulations), and it builds nothing (except its own expansion)."

§

"We have not needed the permission of France, Germany, or the U.N. to act in our generosity, and we do not need it to act in our defense. We are a sovereign nation and, as such, have the right to act in any manner to protect our self-interest. That we welcome the support of just and freedom seeking allies is a reflection of our cooperative spirit, not a required mandate to act."

FOREWORD

In our quest to understand the ramifications of public policy, political rhetoric, and government laws, it helps to have an interpreter. Such a person is Leonard A. Semas. He is a gifted writer. He has passion for the future of our country and he respects our constitutional liberties. The essays that he has penned over the years for the Sierra Sage are priceless and have given me a rich resource for my speaking engagements around the country.

Like many Americans, I am concerned with the liberal direction our country has taken. Our country was founded on a simple concept of freedom. It is freedom we love, respect and fight for. It is freedom we too often take for granted and it is freedom we are slowly losing. Freedom was not given to us by government; it was given by God. Government was created by man to protect that God-given freedom. Although our freedom and liberty are under attack, too many feel helpless to defend, stand up, or express themselves. With *Reason, Justice and Common Sense*, Len Semas speaks for many who care. This book will give readers clear words to help them understand and logically defend our freedoms.

~ Barry M. Goldwater, Jr.

Barry M. Goldwater, Jr. served as a Republican U.S. Congressman from 1969 to 1983, serving northern Los Angeles County. He has a long career in both business and public service, and continues in his writing and speaking to express the passion for his country inspired by his father. The late Senator Barry Goldwater was the Father of Modern Conservatism; his son has accepted the torch of liberty passed on to him and carried it with distinction.

§

INTRODUCTION

About the Sierra Sage

The Sierra Sage is a monthly magazine published in and circulated around Northern Nevada with subscribers throughout the U.S. The Sage is a community publication, with a variety of content and contributors, but its hallmark is its cover essay on politics and contemporary issues.

We are somewhat unique in our attempts to enlighten and provoke. Most "news" oriented publications tend to advocate by stealth. While they claim an unbiased reporting of fact, nothing could be further from the truth. We have no problem with their bias; we just wish they would acknowledge it as such and stop hiding behind a dishonest claim of objectivity. We *are* biased – and we tell you so right up front.

So what is our bias? Is the Sage a "Republican publication?" Well, yes – and no. Is the Sage Conservative? We would say "Constitutional Conservative," but that depends on to whom one speaks.

Our understanding of "reason, justice and common sense," embodies views generally ascribed to Conservatism. In contrast, modern Liberalism derives largely from emotion, without regard to justice and in utter defiance of common sense. Modern Liberals believe that simply "feeling" something is necessary or right is a sufficient basis for its adoption as a desired course – there is no requirement for it to be either reasoned or reasonable.

What about common sense? This is an area that a "regular Joe" can grasp but college professors, politicians, and leading intellects seem unable to. It too, is an essential part of Sage philosophy. It is a recognition of that which is either obvious or absurd on its face. Liberals will require a more extensive definition. Liberals love complication and obfuscation, but neither problems nor solutions are generally as complex as they are made to be. As Einstein observed, "simplicity is the highest form of technology."

The Sage philosophy has other elements beyond its central tenet. A philosophy, to be meaningful, has to be consistent. We strive for consistency as an essential component of logic.

We distinguish between private choices and public policy as an essential aspect of liberty. This is consistent with our constitutional foundations – however eroded in modern law and politics – which support the notions of free choice and limited government. Government does best when it limits itself to public policy on matters delegated to it. It does its worst when it expands beyond that and into the realm of personal choice and private behavior.

We believe that the founders of this Republic were among the brightest men in history, and that they largely "got it right." We take our guidance from the words and intentions of their philosophies expressed in the founding documents These grand works have been trampled by liberal theorists, jurists, politicians, and academics. Our nation will be lost if they are not restored to their rightful place in society.

The Sage philosophy reflects favorably on real solutions; it's not just emotional salve. Feeling good is not doing good; feeding one a fish will never accomplish what teaching one to fish will. It is that simple. We reject the popular calls for bi-partisanship and compromise, as neither provide for real solutions; mostly just feel good solidarity about a middle ground that is neither wholly right nor wholly wrong. Appeasement of two opposing views is not likely to resolve itself to a correct decision, only an acceptable one. Expediency is seldom the road to truth.

The Sage does not publish "train wrecks, car crashes or divorces." We understand the imperfection of man, and the tragedy that accompanies life. We refuse to glorify the tragedy or to dwell on the imperfection. Making a mistake is often punishment itself; we see no value in dragging down people for being human and erring in their lives. The content of "journalism" has become more tabloid-like than ever. We think that demeans both the medium, and the society in which we live. We elect not to join the circus.

The Sage is not defined by dogma or ideology, but by application of fundamental precepts based on our principles. We simply favor the truth – as we see it.

§

About the author

It's instructive to know a bit about me, since the "Sage philosophy," is essentially my philosophy. I've been around since 1947 – a "baby boomer." I grew up in a large family of modest means and humble beginnings. I was taught the virtues of hard work at an early age and have worked since the age of 10. I was also taught basic principles of justice and common sense – reason came later! My parents were married for over 50 years until my dad passed away.

My education included public schools through high school where I played sports, was active in student affairs, and was a college prep student of not especially notable accomplishment. I graduated from a small, private Jesuit school – Santa Clara University. I majored in biology and minored in chemistry and philosophy, the latter a requirement of Jesuit education. I enjoyed the full richness of college life, including the intellectual rigor, development of social skills, and professional level partying.

I volunteered for service in the military, guided by the example of my Dad and others in my family who served in WW II (and motivated by the presence of the "draft"). I entered as a Private and attended Officer Candidate School. I served 3 years during the Viet Nam war, but I was never sent into combat and was honorably discharged as a 1st Lieutenant.

Following the military, I returned to Santa Clara and earned a Master of Business Administration degree, foregoing earlier plans to attend medical school. I spent the next 35+ years in various areas of employment including a stint with a large health care corporation, self employment in the real estate field, and 7 years in a technology company started by my brother. For the past 7 years, I have been the publisher of the Sierra Sage.

The best qualification I can offer to support the publication of my essays and this book, is that I have none of special note. I am simply a "regular" person; one of you.

§

About this book

This book is a compilation of essays published in the Sierra Sage magazine over the past 7 years. The essays have been reorganized according to subject for a more logical flow. As a result, comments and observations that are time related may not be currently relevant as they reflect prior periods. In addition, some issues and ideas may be repeated from one essay to the other, as subject matter may be either similar or overlapping. But such repetitions tend to reflect topics which are considered of utmost importance, such as repeal of the income tax, or dealing with illegal immigration, thus validating their importance.

I believe that we are living in the most critical period in our nation's history since 1776. In my conversations with large numbers of citizens, including many Sierra Sage readers, I believe there is widespread agreement on this. The anger and passion exhibited at Tea Parties and Town Forums around the country are evidence of the frustration. The "Silent Majority" has found its voice - and its reason.

My purpose in pulling together these essays from the Sierra Sage is to give further voice to the sentiments so often expressed. A common and gratifying comment I hear from readers of the Sage is something like, "You write exactly what I think. Thank you for giving my thoughts a place in the public debate."

It is time to spread the word; to widen the debate; to bring America back home to its founding principles and constitutional moorings. It is time to restore reason, justice and common sense.

"If You Would Not Be Forgotten, As Soon As You Are Dead And Rotten, Either Write Things Worth Reading, Or Do Things Worth The Writing."
  - Benjamin Franklin

§

TABLE OF CONTENTS

Chapter 10   Personal Reflections

Epilogue

Mea Culpa

§

CHAPTER 1

AMERICA

"America is great because she is good. If America ceases to be good, America will cease to be great."
~ Alexis de Tocqueville

WHAT IS AMERICA? (JAN 2008)

As we move into another year, yesterday's headlines give us pause. That our press and other media focus on tragedy, failure and shortcomings may leave us with a sense of despair. We often hear that we are the greatest nation in history, yet the headlines suggest otherwise. We receive carping and criticism from around the world for that which we do, or that which we don't. Are we that bad, or do we suffer from an unfounded insecurity complex? Perhaps, we simply forget who we are.

America is not a race or ethnicity, but stands alone as the world's melting pot of all races and ethnicities. More significantly, America is a place where one is neither advanced nor restrained by heritage. True, we bear the historic scars of slavery, though we risked the demise of our nation in a war to end it. While many still dwell in differences, however, the majority of us go about our days dealing with each other as equals; with more in common than not, limited only by our personal choices and actions.

As we enter another election year, many of us – perhaps most – are cynical about the prospects. We have endured decades of a political elite motivated by self-interest and perpetuating their office, rather than limited service for the public good. We hear from politicians of the problems we face – and how government, alone, can fix them. Yet this is not America. America is the handful of "Mr. Smiths" going to Washington and our statehouses, with a sense of duty and a goal of betterment for their fellow citizens through the limited role of governing. America is self-sufficiency, not a nanny state. America is not the politician, but the *statesman*, however few.

Thanks to a morbid fascination with celebrity, America is tainted with an inaccurate portrayal as spoiled, superficial, irresponsible, and given to excess. Britney Spears is an American; America is not Britney Spears. There are far too many Americans that lead lives filled with crime, addiction, abuse, laziness or other human failures. They are Americans - but they are not America.

So what IS America?

America is the millions of moms that lead challenging and fulfilling lives as homemakers or perform work outside the home. Whatever their demands, they find joy in listening to their kids read a story, making sandwiches for the entire neighborhood, volunteering for an endless array of charities, or simply sharing the blessings of a contented home. Many are not paid for all they do, except in smiles and hugs and a knowledge that they are needed and loved.

America is the vast majority of dads that work to provide for their families, fight to defend their country, and provide the necessary anchor in life despite their worries or troubles. They debate the issues of the day out of concern for the future of others, not for themselves. They make time for a day of fishing, a school open house, or a moment for a needed hug. They shoulder their burdens with a stoic shrug and a smile. That's just what they do. They are America.

America is the endless array of kids that stream from classrooms to playgrounds or after-school activities and jobs. They are good, decent, respectful, talented, and kind. Despite a propensity for pushing the edge in fashion, their hearts are innocent. They grow up to attend college, or work in a trade, or to contribute in any manner of ways. They look after their siblings, and their parents in later years, as they become the "next generation." They become the defenders of our nation and our way of life. They serve. For all the concerns we voice in their maturation, they turn out OK.

America is a vast patchwork of friends, neighbors, family, and associates. While it celebrates the individual, it recognizes the power of collaboration among those of like minds, hearts, and spirit. America is working together, socializing together, and achieving together.

America is a nation of immigrants, with one fundamental and common objective: *to be an American.* They come from different cultures and countries to call America home; to adopt its values, to learn its language, and to embrace its beliefs. They come to give all they can, and to take only what they need. They are secure in knowing that freedom and opportunity will bless them beyond their greatest expectations.

America is an army of givers, caretakers, and volunteers, assisting those in need, whether temporary or lifelong. They build that which is needed and rebuild that which is broken. They feed, clothe, and shelter without questioning, judging, or condemning; their hearts are their guides. They perform good deeds through institutions and organizations, or quietly, on their own.

America is a steward of the physical world around it. It is not without failures or mistakes, but it owns up to them and strives to be better. It is mindful of its place in the physical world; mindful of its example to others. It avoids fads and trends for political expediency, preferring the wisdom of science and reason. It constantly works to be better and to create a better world for others – *and it does.*

America is a workplace of dedicated and highly trained contributors in all fields of endeavor. It is a place of creativity and innovation that is the marvel of the world. It produces more, invents more, and contributes more than any nation on earth. It responds to needs, whether natural or man-made, turning challenges into opportunities. It hungers for knowledge, thrives on achievement, and shares its successes with future generations and fellow nations, expecting nothing in return.

America is a protector of fairness and restraint. Despite criticisms to the contrary, both foreign and domestic, it is not an empire builder or a conqueror. It has freed millions from tyranny, saved millions more from hunger, and inspired other millions who were lost. While far from perfect, it is still the beacon of liberty to the world, and who would take its place? Who among its critics would prefer life in a world without it?

America is a spiritual and moral nation. It is a nation founded in a Christian philosophical tradition, while maintaining at least some adherence to those beliefs among the large majority of its citizens. It promotes a tolerance for all belief systems, and for those holding none at all. Saints and sinners are on equal ground, as are atheists, agnostics, and those of all faiths. It protects the right to speak and to believe as private choices dictate, requiring only that our individual actions abide our collective moral principles.

America is, at its core, an idea. It is the embodiment of freedom, created by the reasoned intellect, dedication to principle, and steadfast determination of its founders. Its birth was baptized in the blood of those who placed liberty above all else. They did not yet know the greatness of America, only that which liberty could encourage it to be. They framed that idea in our Declaration of Independence, asserting the fundamental equality and God-given liberty of all men, and the right to institute a government to secure all other rights, as well as to alter or abolish it. The success or failure of that great idea lies in whether each generation lives up to its hallowed canons. The question now is: *Will we?*

§

CHAPTER 2

CRISIS, FEAR AND ANGER

"All that is necessary for the triumph of evil is for good men to do nothing."
    ~ Edmund Burke

AN AMERICAN CRISIS (DEC 2008)

Thomas Paine was 39 when he wrote *The American Crisis* (published December 23, 1776 and continuing in several parts to 1783). The opening line is eerily suggestive of the current state of our country: *"These are the times that try men's souls."* One might argue that at the time of the American Revolution, citizens actually fared better than today. After all, they had but one despot in King George; today, we have 545, representing the three branches of our government. The King had limited contact with the colonists, with enumerated abuses stated in the Declaration of Independence, whereas our government is pervasively present in every aspect of our lives.

It is important to distinguish between our country and our government. America is the greatest country on earth. It is so because of the philosophy under which it was founded and the intrinsic character of the American people. Our government was a creation of the people, in accordance with the provisions of our founding principles and documents, and to be guided by them. *Alas, it is not any longer.* It is, in fact, the most serious threat to our founding principles and has secured for itself far greater resistance to constraint than King George. Government has become a tyrant, not a servant as was intended; it has become ruinous to the liberty of the people, not protective of it. An American crisis once again afflicts our great nation, and we have ignored it far too long.

Not just the economy, Stupid

As we are embroiled in an economic calamity of gigantic proportions, it is tempting to think that *that* is the problem. It is not. It is merely symptomatic of a much broader and deeper disease of long-standing. It has also become an excuse to further leverage the reach of government into our lives and pocket books. Trillions of dollars of Americans' money is being tossed about as if it were small change. Tens of billions for one set of political cronies or another. Justifications based on job losses, financial instability, or hardship are not sufficient reasons for violating the fundamental freedom of Americans.

The Primary Tool of Tyranny

The year 1913 was a watershed for government to commence its path to tyranny. The weapon it created was the income tax. The founders feared taxation on income for good reason; they supported only a tax on consumption (sales tax) or tariffs on foreign goods. Such methods of securing revenue were visible, limited to the intended purpose, and controllable by the citizen-consumers. The income tax, by contrast, set up a means for rewarding or punishing citizens, invading their privacy, and gaining control over them, creating subsidies and penalties, and tinkering in all manners of social engineering. The income tax created the possibility of unrestrained growth of government and uncontrolled violation of the rights of citizens.

Individual freedom and responsibility

Many government programs have been established which rob citizens of their right to provide for themselves or any sense of duty to do so. Among the worst are: retirement, health care, and education. The Social Security Program was set up as a safety net, with limited contribution from all so that the needy few would not be turned out into the streets. What began well intentioned turned into a Ponzi scheme disaster, with an ever-increasing need to fund greater benefits, empowering government as a savior to the recipients. The safety net became a full-fledged retirement program, without individual control or even receiving the benefits paid for, but with an invasive duty to pay, nonetheless.

Health care is rapidly moving in the same direction as social security. Limited emergency care for those unable to pay is morphing into a system where citizens who do pay, directly or through insurance programs, pay huge costs to offset those who don't. Like social security, it is moving toward pure socialism.

Public education seems like an innocent enough concept, except that it is more based on indoctrination than education. It is mistakenly thought of as "free" though in most states it consumes the large majority of state and local budgets, while thirsting for more still. Once again, there is little control over the program or the spending – it is simply taken and consumed as the bureaucrats dictate. Worse, the decisions and dictates are increasingly nationalized, making control or reform impossible. Those who resort to home or private schooling simply pay twice, while still subsidizing the public system for both legal and illegal residents.

Laws and Regulations
No one knows how many laws there are, together with bureaucratic regulations to clarify, administer and enforce them. Suffice it to say that most law-abiding citizens could not leave their homes for a day without breaking one law or another. Like taxes, laws are made not for the legitimate purpose of making us safer or more secure in our liberties. They are made for creating revenue, penalizing enemies or rewarding friends, advancing special agendas, and other purposes having little to do with either justice or safety. The process is made worse by a focus on *creating* laws, never revising, consolidating, or abolishing them. Our legal system does not protect our interests in liberty and justice; it violates or extinguishes them.

Sacrificing Sovereignty
Protection of our borders and our way of life are among the most basic reasons for government to exist. Yet it fails miserably. In 1986 we legalized some 3.6 million people living in our country illegally, only to have the hoards continue to grow to 12-20 million in subsequent years. We continue to permit the entrance into our country of people with cultural

values that compete or even conflict with our own. In the worst cases, we even allow those to come who wish to destroy us.

Under the guise of a huge global warming fraud, we stand prepared to yield significant sovereignty to the U.N. and other international bodies. We are undergoing a gradual shift in our international presence from participation to subjugation. Many believe that is a fine thing.

Anti-Capitalism

We have burdened employers with obligations for personal benefits having nothing to do with the true nature of the enterprise: *to make money*. We have discouraged entrepreneurship and small company innovation by regulation and interference, while at the same time favoring consolidation of large companies into monopolies or oligopolies. We have given special treatment in the form of contracts and subsidies to some, often on the basis of political contributions, not competition and performance. We have entered into trade relationships more beneficial to our trading partners than to our citizens. Our manufacturing, financial, energy, and other needs are so incapacitated that we are vulnerable to and dependent upon other nations. We have allowed lawyers to pursue consumer protection and product liability issues to an idiotic degree, advancing the notion that no one should be responsible for making informed decisions to protect their self-interest.

Attack on Culture

Although we were founded as a nation under Christian philosophy and a respect for our Creator, we have wrongly moved to limit - even deny - such a connection in the public sphere. We have promoted other philosophies and religions at the expense of our own founding belief system. The result has not been to preserve freedom of religious choice, but to promote godlessness or to elevate other cultures above our own. We have succumbed to a gay agenda that promotes aberrant lifestyles to legitimate standing with the natural bond of a man and woman. We have catered to any number of interests that are *special* in nature, at the expense of the *general* welfare, including the forfeiture of our common language.

Nationalism
Great debate and ultimately, compromise, resulted in a governmental system based on Federalism. The delicate balance was part national in character, and part federal, that is, preserving state's rights. The specific intention was to promote to national control those things that best served the people as a whole, such as a national defense. All other rights and duties were to be reserved to the states or to the people themselves. Since 1913, the balance of duties and control has shifted dramatically to *national* control of our lives. Through tortured court decisions, reckless legislation, power grabbing executive orders, and even naïve abandonment of our personal responsibilities, *national* government has come to dominance. The result is an ugly perversion of what the people founded; it is morphing back into King George III.

Moral Justification
Increasingly, money and resources of U.S. citizens is being confiscated for purposes not essential to their well-being, or otherwise constitutionally justified. Foreign aid is given, wars are fought and foreign dictators are assuaged with the money taken from Americans without their consent. The culprit in this violation of citizen's rights is a governmental sense of moral purpose. No such purpose, however, exists - only the need to act constitutionally in our nation's self-interest as expressly empowered. It is the great desire of Liberals, Statists and Internationalists to take *your* money based on *their* perception of goodness or need.

Elite Political Class
Those running government were never intended to be a permanent class, much less a royal one. But they are. The rules of politics, aided by an irresponsible media and a thirst for celebrity has over-ruled a respect for ideas, wisdom, and duty. Thus was Hillary Clinton *crowned* senator, thus is Caroline Kennedy being courted for the same office, and thus does Harry Reid, as we speak, groom his sons for their ascendancy to public life. The rules so favor those in power, the money is so controlled by special interest quid pro quos, and the system so filled with corruption, it is impossible to unseat the insiders. The most transparent political crooks

are lightly punished, while the majority engage in unsavory dealings as a matter of course – and of self-preservation. Public office is sought not to serve the whole, but to benefit the few, with oneself at the top of the list. There is no discernable difference between today's political elite and the royal class under the English king and his aristocracy. *None.*

The Move toward Socialism

Socialism is the ultimate reward for the powerful and the greedy. It advances incrementally by promising more and more to the many to meet their needs; it is a seduction of the lazy, the ill prepared, the gradually indoctrinated, and the weak. It is like the curtain of the Wizard of Oz, behind which those in control live very much different lives. One might ask, if equality among the masses is so great, why is it that the leadership exempt themselves from its benefits? The beneficiaries of monarchies are monarchs and those of socialist systems are the Socialist leaders. Only in a capitalist republic such as ours *used to be* is the individual truly free to rise or fall based on personal choice and accomplishment. When government takes away the freedom to fail, it removes the freedom to succeed as well.

America is in crisis, and it is of our own doing. We have allowed it in small increments, every time government promised to make life better by taking on a role that was not its to take. Government is created or abolished by the people. When government instituted by the people becomes destructive to the purposes for which it was formed, it is the right of the people to alter or abolish it and institute new government to preserve the safety and happiness of the people. *Sound familiar?* This was the basis on which our government was first formed, and its principles are intact still. It remains to be seen whether the people of this great republic will exercise the power granted them by their grand founding documents.

§

A NATION OF FEAR (SEP 2006)

"So, first of all, let me assert my firm belief that the only thing we have to fear is fear itself -- nameless, unreasoning, unjustified terror which paralyzes needed efforts to convert retreat into advance."
        ~ Franklin D. Roosevelt, Inaugural Address, 1933

America, land of the free, home of the brave. Does it still justify that lofty title? We purport to be free but one by one, our liberties are stripped from us by an over-reaching national government. "From the halls of Montezuma, to the shores of Tripoli." So begins the Marine Hymn, and to be sure, the United States Marines and other members of America's armed forces are among the bravest and most fearless on earth. But what about the rest of the country? What of America's children and youth, its regular working folks, its seniors? More than ever all of these people – *all of us* – live more in fear than ever before. Why is this? How is it manifested? How did it happen? What do we do to return to the proud and brave traditions of our history? What are the consequences if we don't?

The biggest culprit driving fear is the mainstream media. For some time now, what they have passed off as "reporting" the news is really nothing more than sensationalizing it. "If it bleeds, it leads," is the motto of the press and television news media. And it leads for weeks on-end. Then there are the follow-ups, the speculative "expert" interviews, and the surveys (invariably skewed to be as fear provoking as possible).

According to Paul Klite, late Executive Director of Rocky Mountain Media Watch (RMMW), "Murder, one of the least common crimes, is the number one topic on newscasts." According to the group Children Now, while the homicide rate dropped 33 percent during the period between 1990 and 1998, news coverage of homicides actually increased by 473 percent. An RMMW study of local TV newscasts across the country shows that 40 to 50 percent of all news airtime is devoted to violent topics.

If the "news" end of the media is fear mongering, the entertainment side is no better. Television and movies tend to focus on fear as entertainment, whether criminal, "documentary," or disaster. A better balance between violence, comedy, heroic action, history, and romance would go along way to balance our fears. Especially troubling is the steady stream of fear oriented programs and games promoted to young people.

Our legal system has done much to facilitate a climate of fear. We have lost the concepts of accidents, oversights, and simple mistakes. Every action or inaction must be accompanied by legal sanctions and penalties creating a fear to simply live life and accept its consequences. The political system (largely the waste water of our legal system) has promoted the same mind set: every success is at someone's expense; every failure creates a class of victims who must be protected - even rewarded - as compensation for their failure or loss.

Childhood used to be a time of joy and discovery; a gradual acquisition of freedom to roam about and experience an ever-expanding world. Not anymore. Kids are tethered to moms or dads with physical leashes so they won't wander off, or equipped with cell phones in the event they do. Reporting in to the home base is constant. Forget about a free ranging neighborhood of pals to explore with and critters to explore: *there are pedophiles out there waiting to pounce, and worse, kidnappers and murderers.* You think school is safe? Remember Columbine – it could happen to you. No toys either, especially cap or BB guns; they can lead to violence or get you killed. No "cops and robbers;" no "cowboys and Indians;" and certainly no simulated army battles – these can all result in violence, or - *shudder* – may even offend someone! Just to be sure the little ones are safe, we'll have them fingerprinted and implanted with an electronic chip. Oh yeah, no Hostess cupcakes, Twinkies, or soft drinks – obesity is epidemic among kids!

So you somehow survive childhood with a few jitters, but otherwise intact. Thinking about a relationship? AIDS and STDs are out there just waiting for you. Thinking of marriage? Forget it – more than half of them end in divorce. Perhaps some prayer and reflection would help? I don't think so – *pedophile priests.* You'd like a commitment but there is that fear of failure. Life is not getting any easier. Someday you'll get old. Will Medicare be there? Social Security?

Maybe you'll find some solace and satisfaction in the workplace. Guess again. Pay a lady a compliment on her nice dress and you're courting a sexual harassment charge. Fail to hire the right color, gender, sexual orientation – *lawsuit*. Comment unthinkingly about a new product or company contract – uh oh, you're in trouble with the SEC. In fact, compliance with the law is so overwhelming, you can forget about what's *right* – just do what is *legal*... or face the consequences. Yup – no reason to be fearful in the workplace.

Certainly being out in public among people must be free from fear – we live in a safe and healthy country, right? Nope. There are illegal immigrants taking your jobs and your culture, gangs and rapists in the cities. There are terrorists on every plane, ship, and train waiting to blow you up and feed you anthrax or use some other bio-terror weapon. Maybe it's safer in the country or small towns? You wish. Ever heard about Swine Flu, Asian Bird Flu or West Nile Virus? And don't touch that hamburger – Mad Cow Disease!

Can you be fear free anywhere? No – not really. West Coast? Earthquakes. East Coast? Hurricanes. Midwest? Tornadoes!

The reality is that danger, disease, and disaster lurk everywhere. Freedom from fear is not a place; it is a state of mind. More and more we are allowing ourselves to live in fear, ultimately because we choose to. It is the nature of modern media and entertainment to subliminally encourage us to, and of terrorists who actively want us to. When we conform, we elevate the media beyond their significance and we surrender to terrorists our liberty. Neither condition is acceptable in a free society.

Our belief in a good God and in a just society will give us comfort in tackling a world that is full of danger, death, and disease, but it is our right to *choose* that is the final arbiter of whether we live in freedom or in fear. Our personal and collective strength as a nation will allow us to make the that choice; weakness will surrender it. Which path will we follow?

§

I'M AS MAD AS HELL
And I'm not going to take this anymore *(MAR 2009)*

"When the people fear their government, there is tyranny; when the government fears the people, there is liberty."
  ~ Thomas Jefferson

P eter Finch as Howard Beale in the 1976 movie "Network:" *"I don't have to tell you things are bad. Everybody knows things are bad. It's a depression. Everybody's out of work or scared of losing their job. The dollar buys a nickel's worth; banks are going bust; shopkeepers keep a gun under the counter; punks are running wild in the street, and there's nobody anywhere who seems to know what to do, and there's no end to it.*

We know the air is unfit to breathe and our food is unfit to eat. And we sit watching our TVs while some local newscaster tells us that today we had fifteen homicides and sixty-three violent crimes, as if that's the way it's supposed to be!

We all know things are bad -- worse than bad -- they're crazy.

It's like everything everywhere is going crazy, so we don't go out any more. We sit in the house, and slowly the world we're living in is getting smaller, and all we say is, "Please, at least leave us alone in our living rooms. Let me have my toaster and my TV and my steel-belted radials, and I won't say anything. Just leave us alone."

Well, I'm not going to leave you alone.

I want you to get mad!

I don't want you to protest. I don't want you to riot. I don't want you to write to your Congressman, because I wouldn't know what to tell you to write. I don't know what to do about the depression and the inflation and the Russians and the crime in the street. All I know is that first, you've got to get mad.

You've gotta say, "I'm a human being, goddammit! My life has value!"

So, I want you to get up now. I want all of you to get up out of your chairs. I want you to get up right now and go to the window, open it, and stick your head out and yell, 'I'm as mad as hell, and I'm not going to take this anymore!!'"

In this impassioned diatribe, the fictitious Howard Beale gave voice 30 years ago to the same frustration and helpless feelings experienced by Americans today.

Through its first 175 years, this great nation functioned well. It flourished through the early to mid-20th century. America became the beacon of freedom throughout the world. Nations were made prosperous by American enterprise and made better through American inventiveness and creativity. Whole nations were freed or saved by the intervention of American military might, and the sacrifice of selfless millions who fought not just for their own freedom, but for that of millions more around the globe. American success in agriculture fed the hungry while advances in science and medicine struck down one disease after another. The American educational system lifted all intellects, from modest to brilliant, and the spirit of the American character provided an example for hard work and successful living.

From our earliest times, the seminal principles of our Declaration of Independence were held sacred and the preeminent authority of our Constitution was ironclad. The symbolism of our flag was universally respected and the allegiance of all to their nation was unquestioned. It was not considered deficient for a man to act like one, nor a woman to value her femininity and the blessings of motherhood.

The downhill slide that has taken hold of us in a mere half-century should make us all angry; it should make us *mad as hell*. It is inexcusable and unexplainable except for one thing: **government**. Our government is not America; it is a creation of the people who *are*. We have allowed the transformation of a servant into a monster.

The original concept was simple, basic – even benign. We would take the states we had created for the purpose of societal necessity and combine them into a single confederation for purposes of greater security and protection, and to assume our standing among the world of nations. The states would be the primary repository for laws affecting our daily lives while the new federal government would take care of interstate and international issues. It would address matters of state conflicts, national defense and the general welfare and happiness of the citizens. It would facilitate commerce and trade with other nations, provide for orderly immigration of new residents and make laws necessary for its limited functions. It would be funded though consumption (sales) taxes and duties on foreign goods. A simple concept: *the powers not granted to the federal government would be reserved to the states and the citizens*. A simple goal: *life, liberty, and the pursuit of happiness*.

We are no longer a confederation of states; we no longer have a federal government. We have a national monstrosity that usurps every power within its grasp and sucks the lifeblood of every citizen, state, and enter-prise for its own ever-growing expansion. We have made a mockery of the "rule of law" so essential to our Republic by passing millions of them, thereby depriving the law of having any legitimate meaning or basis for justice. We have compounded the weight of excessive law with the complexity of endless regulation and bureaucracy. We should be mad as hell we have allowed this travesty of justice and invasion of freedom.

The impact of the national beast we have spawned is devastating and insidious; its reach extends into all aspects of our lives. What was created to improve and protect us is destroying and consuming us. The defense from our enemies has itself *become* the enemy.

Consider ~

• Our economy is in shambles. The entrepreneur that created America's economic and technological greatness has been shackled by regulation and taxation. The system of capitalism that rewarded success has been reduced to socialist meddling and the preservation of bloated corporate leviathans motivated by greed and paid-for power, not successful operation or superior products and services.

• Leadership is non-existent. Debate has been mollified in favor of the more innocuous "bi-partisanship." Self-interest and perpetuation of office have replaced the ideal of service for the public good. Our "leaders" have become wealthy in material gain, and impoverished in character. There is more concern for the people in some third-world dictatorships than in the whole of Washington D.C. We are governed by a single party: *the party of government.*

• Personal responsibility has been co-opted. Our responsibilities to our families, our communities, our institutions – even to ourselves – have all been assumed by an over-reaching government that knows better our needs, wants, and duties. There are no accidents, no failures, no unful-filled dreams – only victims and villains. If we can't afford a college education, someone must pay. If we are injured, someone must pay. If we don't have a digital television converter, someone must pay for one. If we are hungry, we don't work harder or grow our food – we demand that someone feed us. We have been reduced by government to beggars and slaves. *Where there are no duties, there are no rights.*

• States have been reduced to irrelevant whores with a national government as their pimp. They sacrifice their sovereign standing for national handouts. When they spend irresponsibly they look to Congress to bail them out. When natural disaster hits, they declare national emergency, not state responsibility (having set aside no funds to deal with such matters). When the national government interferes in their legitimate powers, they bow to it rather than assert their constitutional rights. In good times they spend all they have; in bad times they simply confess a "need" to confiscate more. One might question why they even exist except, perhaps, for promoting tourism and issuing proclamations.

• An Aristocracy has replaced the Republic. As Orwell wrote in *Animal Farm*, "... all pigs are created equal, but some are more equal than others." The distance and insulation of our elected representatives from the people, the corruption of the political system, and the influence of money and special interests, have combined to created an elite class. Politicians move at ease with celebrities and corporate money-mongers. They live in a world of private jets, international travel, the finest of food and clothing, and palatial residences. They are not "Harry Trumans." Worse, they are perfectly content with their fantasy self-image of "serving the people."

I could go on.

Americans live in fear of their government. It has become a many-headed Hydra, with each of its poisonous tentacles extending into the lives of citizens, aggregating more of its own power at the expense of their freedoms. Like the Hydra, each time one of its heads is cut off, three new ones appear. The solution is, as Hercules discovered, to vanquish the monster in its entirety.

There is no internal solution. Term limits are laughed at; reforms and reinventions are laughable. Each time government claims to deal with its flaws, it emerges worse from the futile exercise. Each flawed generation of politicians passes the torch of power to its offspring, its financial backers and its fellow crooks. Those few brave souls who enter with a sense of duty and purity in their hearts are soon corrupted by the fatally flawed system, and their own character withers into compliance.

Only the gangs run free. They control the cities at night as fearful, law-abiding citizens seeking only freedom and happiness retreat into their living rooms to watch more of the political circus on the evening news. The gangs feel empowered, the people feel powerless; their only outlet is the conversation shared among the like-minded at the local coffee shop or corner bar. What can they do?

They can get angry.

When government exceeds the purpose for which it was created; when a political elite thumbs its collective nose at the people for whom they serve; when life, liberty, and the pursuit of happiness is impaired by those granted power to secure it, the people have only to look to themselves for resolution and repair.

Much is made of the Constitution as the supreme law of the land, and a supremely elegant guide to governing it is. But there is a document that takes precedence even over our grand Constitution. The Declaration of Independence is what defined our right to separate from England, and it framed the basis for the relationship between a people and the government they created. The rights of the people to institute government among themselves is God granted, not government permitted. When people get sufficiently angry; when 10 million rise up to reclaim and restore government, *as is their right*, only then will we have a chance to return our country to greatness.

But first, we must get mad – mad as hell.

The solution will follow.

§

CHAPTER 3

CRUMBLING INSTITUTIONS
God

"Our Constitution was made only for a moral and religious people. It is wholly inadequate to the government of any other."
~ *John Adams*

REJECTION OF GOD AND MORAL LAW (MAY 2003)

One nation under God. In God we trust. So help me God. Our belief in God is firmly rooted in our daily lives: our national pledge, our coins and currency, and the oaths we take. On that tragic day of September 11, 2001, our leaders invoked the name of God to help heal, understand, and protect this great nation. As we embarked on the effort to free the people of Iraq and remove power from its evil dictator, our military, leaders, and citizens all appealed to the Almighty for guidance and for support in our just efforts. How is it then that God and the moral law that derives from our Judeo-Christian heritage is under attack in so many quarters? This is not about personal morality, it is about the structure of our nation; one historically and culturally based on the God that we increasingly secularize.

As stated in the preamble of our Constitution, the Godly character of our country was established: to *"...secure the Blessings of Liberty to ourselves and our Posterity."* Note this wasn't simply a *grant* of liberty, but a *blessing*. Having defined this essential purpose, the Framers then added a caveat: *"Congress shall make no law respecting an establishment of religion, or prohibiting the free exercise thereof."* This distinction between rights granted by God and the exercise of those rights through a chosen religious preference has been abused to undermine our culture, and our system of morality. The ACLU, numerous courts, and many misguided individuals have tortured the intent of our founders in their wailing for a "separation of church and state." To be sure, we are not a nation of Catholics, or Protestants, or Baptists, though all are included among us – but we are very much a nation of God. That fact is being stripped away in little increments, and it is having a catastrophic effect on our families, our communities, and our culture as a whole.

John Quincy Adams remarked that *"The highest glory of the American Revolution was this; it connected, in one indissoluble bond the principles of civil government with the principles of Christianity."* Can that statement be construed in any other manner than the obvious? The Pilgrims, our first settlers, challenged an ocean as broad then as a universe now to establish a way of life free from religious persecution – but based on the moral and civil laws of nature's God; a Christian God. This distinction between religion and Godliness served our country well for most of its first 200 years. It provided the basis for our family and community values, the moral component of our legal and governmental systems and the ultimate guide for our personal behavior, however each of us might fall short. It required tolerance of other belief systems, but established the values and culture of our own. Unlike some countries in the world, the preservation of our own faith did not require the rejection, or even destruction, of that of others.

On the verge of collapse of the Constitutional Convention in June of 1787, a frail Benjamin Franklin had the following remarks read on his behalf: *"In the beginning of the contest with Britain, when we were sensible of danger, we had daily prayers in this room for Divine protection. Our prayers, Sir, were heard and they were graciously answered. All of us who were engaged in the struggle must have observed frequent instances of a superintending Providence in our favor. . . . And have we now forgotten this powerful Friend? Or do we imagine we no longer need His assistance?"* The speech marked a turning point in the convention, and with a renewed sense of faith, Congress returned to opening daily sessions with a prayer. How strange that a Constitution was forged in the atmosphere of prayer, and now we remove it from schools, and most every aspect of public life.

A continuing progression down the path of materialism, secularism and "feel good" justifications has watered down our sense of personal moral duty. In the past 50 years, a plethora of rights have been established, while the responsibilities and obligations of citizenship have been steadily diminished. From small infringements such as a loss of manners and civility, to our very respect for life, rights have supplanted duties, until the latter are unrecognizable.

A major component in the moral decline has been the confusion, not unintentional, of private versus public behaviors. Our interest as a nation is served when we encourage the formation and growth of stable, traditional families, including responsibility toward our children as well as our parents. Those values are also supported by the moral dictates of our Judeo-Christian philosophy. In recent years, however, the trend has been to sanction acceptable public behaviors on the basis of personal ones, which may conflict with the public moral good. Private behavior between consenting adults may be subject only to personal religious beliefs, moral convictions, or simply choice. But that does not compel the public, nor does it serve the public interest, to require tolerance or acceptance of such behavior as a matter of public policy. It is this distinction that is increasingly under attack, and which sacrifices the moral rights of one group to another. Common sense and public values are sacrificed at this alter of political correctness.

The attack on God and public morality has been greatly assisted by the loss of community and state-level values formerly protected by federalism. The more distant from the citizens, the easier it is to usurp their basic rights and values. The more consolidated the power of our government, the less answerable it is to society as a whole and the more malleable to special interests with solid voting blocks and financial support. Thomas Jefferson was prescient in this at the outset: *"the true theory of our Constitution is surely the wisest and best . . . (for) when all government . . . shall be drawn to Washington as the centre of all power, it will render powerless the checks provided of one government on another, and will become as . . . oppressive as the government from which we separated."* That power shift has been largely accomplished through activist court decisions, a permanent class of politicians, abuse of executive authority, and constitutional tampering.

Our local schools are loathe to stop a federal agenda that is motivated by indoctrination and political correctness, rather than basic values, the transference of knowledge, and the development of critical thinking. Public education has become *government indoctrination*, and beyond its costliness, it is ineffectual and valueless. Special interests of every stripe are elevated in their own agendas, no matter what rights, values, or preferences exist for others not of their persuasion. The right to even *hold* opinions inconsistent with the aims of those groups is under attack, despite "free speech" provisions that tolerate the burning of our nation's flag or the desecration of religious - at least Christian - symbols. The "god" we pay homage to today is the *national* government – it controls the purse strings, harasses and punishes the "infidels" who question its moral authority, and sets the agenda for all things affecting our daily lives. The "mainstream" has become perverted to mean that which is acceptable in Washington D.C., Manhattan, or Hollywood – not Midland, Texas. While our own Godly heritage is under attack and dilution, that of other cultures is being accommodated beyond reason. A Christian child may not bring a bible to school for fear of offending someone, but a Muslim woman in Florida is allowed to obtain a driver's license with her ID photo obscured by a veil.

Our modern values celebrate women in traditional male roles as an achievement of equality - but at the expense of respect for women in their own traditional roles and motherhood, in particular. Why can't we celebrate both?

We call them entertainment, but "reality" shows simply demonstrate the depths to which people will sink. Human dignity can be bought or sold, seems to be the message - and cheaply at that. Our families continue to disintegrate, yet the response of those governing society is to suggest a "village" as a replacement, to offer yet more hours of public day care, and to tax families into submission with mothers working in careers that come before kids.

Victimhood is elevated and criminal acts are explained away by one psychosis or another. We have difficulty executing a 17-year-old guilty of horrific murders, yet kill innocent unborn children, and justify it as a "right to choose." Criminals and illegal aliens receive free education, food, clothing, shelter, recreation and more, and yet hard working middle-class Americans struggle for the same basic needs. Rights are absolute, yet morality is relative.

Something is terribly wrong with this picture and the diminishment of Godly values in our culture is at the core of it all.

One wonders if it is too late to turn back, but we must try.

So help us God.

§

CRUMBLING INSTITUTIONS
The Family

"Families must continue to be the foundation of our nation. Families—not government programs—are the best way to make sure our children are properly nurtured, our elderly are cared for, our cultural and spiritual heritages are perpetuated, our laws are observed and our values are preserved.

Thus it is imperative that our government's programs, actions, officials and social welfare institutions never be allowed to jeopardize the family.

We fear the government may be powerful enough to destroy our families; we know that it is not powerful enough to replace them."
~ Ronald Reagan

MOMS & DADS (MAR 2005)

Andrea Yates methodically killed her five children. Susan Smith drowned her two young sons in a seemingly unfeeling act. Countless other children have suffered pain, injury, and death at the hands of their own mothers and fathers. These stories make the front pages, but the strains facing even normal moms and dads are there too. These parents cope, but not without headache, heartache, anguish, and stress. Before parents can get a grip, society needs to come to grips with this challenge to its cornerstone: *the family.*

Families are increasingly torn apart with mom, dad or both missing from children's lives. Even in divorces where both parents remain involved, too often there is one primary parent trying to play both roles while the other is too busy with other priorities to care. Both financial support and personal support are often missing, placing extra strains on the parent that remains involved. Children require a loving, caring and responsible mom *and* dad in their lives. That is how nature intended things. Anything less takes even greater effort, time, and financial resources to repair and deal with the problems of separation. Unfortunately, it is usually less of these things – not more – that is the reality for most families.

Society needs to raise its demands upon parents to provide for the needs of children they have produced. The right to reproduce is not without responsibilities, and once a child results from a parental union, those responsibilities need to be primary – even at the expense of inconvenience, discomfort, or pain caused to the parents. Parents – *both parents* – may not have that new car at the expense of their child's needs; they may not have their evenings and weekends free to date, relax or travel; they may have to forego bowling night to attend the school open house; and they may have to arrange their lives so that the reasonable needs of their children are met. The laws and the courts need to insist on this, and the stigma of peers and the community must be enlisted to shame parents, if necessary, into compliance. *Duties to our children are not optional.*

It is heartbreaking to witness single parents – usually mothers – struggling to balance the demands of working, maintaining a livable home, dealing with school needs, transporting kids to events and activities of all kinds, fixing meals, healing wounds, and still finding time and strength to love, nurture, and understand – *alone*. Raising kids as a couple is a challenge, to be sure; doing it alone is stressful beyond belief, though dutifully carried out by most single parents. Parents who excuse themselves from their kid's lives are simply shameful. They are shameful for the loss they create in the children themselves, and for the strain they place on the custodial parent who carries on the duties of parenthood. Such callous behavior should not be tolerated by anyone – friends, family or society at large.

Schools are both part of the solution and part of the problem. They take up some of the slack in providing meals that harried single parents are challenged to provide; they provide a safe (usually) haven and learning environment while mom or dad is working; and they offer (usually) love and caring from dedicated teachers that serve as extended family. Schools also, unfortunately, can undermine traditional parenting values; they can interfere with parental consent and involvement; and they too often fail in meeting the essential goal of educating our youth for achievement in life. The PTA used to be the means for reconciling the needs of parents and kids in the educational environment – now it is the Washington D.C. bureaucrats and teacher's unions.

Hollywood and pop culture used to play a supportive role in childhood development, and provided examples that could be admired and emulated. Ozzie and Harriet – whatever their off screen life – created an ideal of warmth, caring, and responsible behavior among kids, parents and their environments. Today's kids get television's invariably dysfunctional "families" as their model. Yesterday's athletes – Ted Williams, Bob Cousey, Willie Mays – represented honest competition, duty to God and country, and a wholesome appearance that guided others to follow. Today's sports "heroes" showcase drugs, tattoos, nose rings, and criminal activities, including spousal abuse – and get paid millions for their efforts. Old time westerns and war movies celebrated good over evil and dealt with violence as an unfortunate tool of last resort; today's video games and music videos parade gross violence with graphic indifference to sensibilities in a dehumanizing stream of pure garbage. Being a mom or dad in today's world is a challenge to *finding* innocence, much less supporting it.

Shopping for clothes used to be a pretty simple task for parents – and reasonably affordable. For boys: a couple of pair of jeans (a little long to "grow into" and folded at the cuff in the meantime), a couple of neatly collared plaid shirts, some white socks and underwear, and some soon to be scuffed up shoes. For girls: skirts, sweaters, shirts with sweetly embroidered messages, and "Mary Janes" or white tennies. Today's parents have a hard time finding pants for boys that don't fall off their "behinds," make their daughters look like little "Lolitas," or simply cost an arm and a leg. Kids clothes are fashion statements, rather than simply something functional to wear. Clothing a kid is not easy in today's world – and clothing manufacturers are part of the problem.

Parents spend less time with their kids, and are more fearful of the risks of kidnapping, assault or worse – the stress making it impossible to enjoy time apart, and the demands of work and other needs making it difficult to spend time together. The response is video cameras in the preschool and cell phones in kindergarten. These do not provide personal attention – simply surveillance. The stress does not go away with electronic devices filling in for parental supervision and contact.

In earlier times, when mom and dad couldn't be around, one of the other siblings was; and if they weren't, Grandma or Grandpa was. When they weren't, friends and neighbors known to to the family were. Kids were seldom at a loss for a companion, a game of checkers, or a story. Today, grandparents are touring the country in their RV – or shuttled off to a retirement or nursing home. Siblings are fewer or absent all together as the time demanded in raising children is too difficult to accomodate, or requires other sacrifices many adults are simply unwilling to make. Kids too often have nowhere to turn, and parents too often look the other way or are stressed at their inability to do all they want and need to do.

Moms and dads – and custodial single parents in particular – are stretched thin these days – often to the breaking point. It's a tragedy for society, and it is a special and personal tragedy for the children affected. It has to change. A generation of kids – *our future* – hangs in the balance.

§

CRUMBLING INSTITUTIONS
The Community

"We are a nation of communities... a brilliant diversity spread like stars, like a thousand points of light in a broad and peaceful sky."
  ~ George W. Bush

THE DECLINE OF FAMILY AND COMMUNITY (FEB 2003)

Why is family so important? According to Patrick F. Fagan, writing in the 2003 Policy Makers Briefing Book for the Heritage Foundation, "The family is the building block of society. It is the organism through which the very life of a nation is nurtured on to future generations. Without stable marriages as the basis of the family unit, this organism is weakened, and children are the most seriously affected. Thus, future generations of Americans will bear the brunt of the family's weakness today." If the family is the building block, then local communities are the foundation upon which the rest of society is built. As the Heritage research shows, and as common sense tells us, the building blocks are crumbling and the foundation is shaky:

The environment that allows children to thrive the most is provided by the natural family, consisting of a "mother and father, living together to care for the children they bring into existence," according to the Heritage study. The same source reports that the natural family is also the safest place, while the most dangerous for both a woman and her children is the woman living with a boyfriend. The study notes, "... 1/3 of all children are born out of wedlock, and much more often to adult women than to teens." Heritage goes on documenting excessive divorce or unmarried families and juvenile crime, birth mortality, and poverty all negatively affected. The bottom line is that a strong family is built on "wedlock, worship, and work," all of which seems obvious to most, and all of which seems, sadly, to be in decline.

Communities, too, function best with similar positive influences, and suffer from the negative consequences of crime, welfare, unstable families, and a lack of morality signaled by a decline of religious influences upon which morals and positive values are based. An erosion of common culture is an added factor, as American communities are increasingly divided by ethnic and racial differences; differences that are showcased and favored, rather than assimilation into the "melting pot" that is America's legacy.

While there are many influences on the decline of families and communities, much of the fault has to be placed on the actions and policies of government, including the courts and our public education system. Each of these has contributed to undermining personal responsibility, extending rights beyond reason, diminishing the presence of our faith in God, and in particular, our Judeo-Christian heritage, and in taxing motherhood into the necessity of work outside the home.

There was a time when "community standards" were the determining factor in the moral climate of a community. If a city or town felt that x-rated movies or similar businesses were undesirable, they were not permitted. There was a time when the local PTA had an active and vocal participation in the curriculum and operation of the school educational climate, including moral values, ethics, health, and safety issues. Today, courts are telling schools that they can't expel students for bad behavior; that they must teach condom use and homosexuality as an *alternative* lifestyle; that pregnant teens can continue to attend classes; and that illegal residents cannot be denied attendance in public schools. The educational establishment has lost sight of its mission and become a money-grubbing machine much like the social services "system," in which welfare is a way of life, rather than a safety net; where personal responsibility is not a factor, but multiple, out-of- wedlock births are.

Public entertainment has devolved from the wholesome family oriented shows of the 1950s to the trash that has become the new standard, replete with foul language and the intellectual stupor of drug numbed minds. Television has denigrated all semblance of civility and human dignity, reducing acceptable behavior to publicity and economics. There have always been some people who would do virtually anything for money – they just weren't made into celebrities for it. The music industry, the rest of Hollywood, and their corporate backers aren't any better. The lowest forms of life are celebrated, with losers and gang-like characters becoming the staple of ads oriented to kids; honesty, decency, and wholesome appearance are invisible anachronisms.

In homage to the objective of "diversity," every television show includes a homosexual character, one member of each race, a bumbling white male, and an "I am women" super-mom, usually divorced, who has it all (all but character, that is). Few, if any of us, live in that neat, politically correct packaging of diversity. This is the climate of community championed by the Liberal mindset. It's a world the way they want to see it; not the world the way it exists.

Government, especially at the federal level, has grown to overshadow all aspects of life, inculcating the values of mindless bureaucrats with an agenda contrary to all that is good and wholesome. A *national* education establishment doles out dollars to local schools – with strings attached. A *national* immigration establishment insists that illegal residents receive health, welfare, and education benefits at a huge cost to local communities. Communities either comply, or lose funds from the *national* government. Federal courts – notably the 9th Circuit – undermine all Godly values, forcing removal of the Ten Commandments from public buildings, and references to God from the Pledge of Allegiance. Activists are working on, and succeeding, in removing the Pledge of Allegiance as a condition of citizenship, allowing new citizens to "pledge" their allegiance to their homeland, or Allah, or, presumably, whatever deity or institution meets with their desires.

Children are placed into day care – with the government picking up the tab. Now government is pushing preschool, full-day kindergarten, and after-school child care at taxpayer expense, and to the further detriment of family cohesiveness. Children spend more time away from parents and other family and more with government institutions. Elderly grandparents are considered a burden, and an ever-expanding government at all levels requires both parents to keep working simply to stay in place. There is no money, and therefore no time, for family – thanks to a greedy, socialist, arrogant, imperial state! We are drowning in government "assistance," and still the politicians and bureaucrats think that "they" are the answer. "Newsflash" to D.C. and 50 American statehouses: *You are the problem!*

The answers are not simple, but far from impossible to implement:
• Reduce government spending, and constitutionally limit it, to a fraction of what it presently is, so that people – families – can keep what is earned by one parent for their family needs.
• Create an honest, visible, and fair system of taxation for the greatly reduced demands of government: a sales tax at national and state levels, and no other tax!
• Make personal responsibility – not an ever-growing expanse of rights, the objective of social behavior.
• Return community standards of morality and decency to community control.
• Restore a culture of laws and social stigma, which rewards positive behavior, and discourages immoral and irresponsible behavior.
• Return our historic American traditions, unity, and principles.

The real solution, of course, has to come not from the distant halls of government, but from the people from whom government's power is derived. The excesses of government will never be reined in except by the citizens who have silently allowed their families, communities, and culture to be usurped. They, and they alone, will have to take them back.

§

CRUMBLING INSTITUTIONS
The Nation

"The plan of the [Constitutional] convention aims only at a partial union or consolidation, the State governments would clearly retain all the rights of sovereignty which they before had, and which were not, by that act, exclusively delegated to the United States."
~ *Alexander Hamilton*

FEDERALISM (JAN 2007)

During George Washington's presidency, there were 4 cabinet level offices: War, Treasury, State and Attorney General. Today, there are 15. It is not simply the complexity of the federal level of government which has given rise to this expansion, but a vastly broadened power and domain – at the expense of state and local governments, and of the citizens themselves. *Federalism is in crisis.*

At our country's founding, the *state* was the center of government. With the adoption of the Constitution, the "Confederacy" - a confederation of states - yielded to a power sharing arrangement in which the sovereign states created a new federal level of government for express and limited purposes. Alas, two centuries later, the child has become the parent; the student has become the teacher; and the servant has become the master.

There was sufficient reason for the states to agree to the creation of a consolidated federal government, the most important being the protection of the fledgling states against outside forces – there was safety in numbers and in a unified front. There were justifiable concerns, however, and for that reason, the powers of the new federal government were expressly defined and limited by the 10th Amendment: *"The powers not delegated to the United States by the Constitution, nor prohibited by it to the States, are reserved for the States respectively, or to the people."*

The express powers were largely spelled out in Article 1, Section 8 of the Constitution, and dealt with issues of finance and commerce, national stability and uniformity, national defense, and establishment of a national seat of government. Virtually all other power was to remain with the states and the citizens. This was the essence of federalism.

There are many factors that favor the residence of power at the state, local, and individual levels: visibility and proximity, checks and balances, accountability, creativity and innovation, and protection against abuse by the people's power to more easily remove offenders from office.

Of course, the fundamental nature of freedom and liberty as God-given rights constitutes the basis for all other government grants of authority. Both freedom and responsibility should remain to the greatest extent possible with the individual citizens and their families. The individual and family have, instead, become the weakest elements in the modern hierarchy of power.

The separation of power between the states and the federal government was an important part of the checks and balances sought by our founding fathers; similar to the sharing of power between the executive, legislative, and judicial branches. Increasingly, this separation has become a myth, if not a joke. There is virtually no element of life into which the modern *national* government does not reach: education, school lunch programs, speed limits, drinking and driving, and the list goes on.

The usual route for federal influence starts with money. Congress collects more and more money from the citizens, creates new agencies and involvements and then makes the states dependent on the continued flow of a limited return of money in exchange for compliance with the federal mandates. It is no less than extortion by the federal government – and prostitution by the weak willed states. The new game is to provide "block grants" to the states whereby the states can be bought into submission as a general rule, rather than in response to specific federal compliances. Few states have the fortitude to challenge this intrusion into their constitutional domain so it continues on.

The judiciary has been a willing accomplice in the power grab by the federal government, citing the Commerce Clause, "equal protection," and other liberal interpretations or constructions of the Constitution to assist the federal government extending its reach into virtually every aspect of American life. *Since 1937, not a single Act of Congress has been voided by the Supreme Court as an excess of the Commerce Clause.*

With the ever-increasing concentration of power in Washington, D.C., the distance from the people increases both geographically and philosophically. The "Beltway" becomes a place foreign to the interests of Americans, and in fact, evolves into its own culture and system of special treatment for those who populate it – elected politicians, appointed bureaucrats, and lobbyists. There can be neither familiarity with the real needs of citizens nor accountability to them with such a gulf between the governing and the governed.

Many of our primary institutions are hopelessly broken. The health care and education systems used to function reasonably well. Fifty years of increasing national government involvement parallels the dismal condition into which both have sunk. Is there a connection? Clearly there is, as Jefferson knew there would be. Tinkering by a federal leviathan in the daily affairs of society is an affront to creative solutions and an invitation to bloated bureaucracy. Yet modern politicians want more. National politicians want more power, and state and local ones want the easy life of more federal money. They actually seem relieved of the duty to justify raising taxes, leaving the job to the feds and simply getting their fees through the back door. They are not only incompetent – they are gutless.

The "national" solution is invariably the same – more money, more regulation, more bureaucracy, fewer rights or options. There is no innovation; there is no creativity. Innovation takes place when there are many models simultaneously working, where the best can be compared and emulated, while the worst are rejected. Such an environment works when solutions are decentralized to states and local governments, not when they are held captive in an unimaginative national black hole. In such a place, the best is never sought and the worst finds permanence as the "offspring" of one bureaucrat or another. Such is the basis for the ridiculous "No Child Left Behind" sham.

When control is centralized rather than distributed, the power for indoctrination and abuse becomes absolute. In the education system, such potential for abuse has filtered down to the primary grades. Now there are calls for more governmental involvement in kindergarten and even preschool. The power to fund is, as always, the starting point – the ability to control and indoctrinate derives from a surrender of that duty. Social engineering and values indoctrination are now well established from kindergarten to college. It's little wonder that recent generations look to government more and more and cherish their traditional duties and rights less and less. The brainwashing will continue as long as control remains with national government!

These are but a few examples of the perverse and pervasive influence wielded by Washington today. One of the worst fears of the Founders – a national, rather than a federal government – has become a reality. Returning to the original intentions will not come easily. Every time a senator or congressmen proudly boasts of the federal money he brought back home, he will be contributing to the problem. Every time a governor acquiesces to – or even requests – a new federal program, he will exacerbate the problem. Each call for the federal government to step in and "do something" will result in less freedom and choice for the states – and for the citizens. This is a misguided bargain down the road to tyranny. An all-powerful national government is no less capable of despotism than the most evil of kings. Wake up people. The sands of time are fleeting.

§

THE REPUBLIC
...Needs Fixing *(JUL 2008)*

"I pledge allegiance to the Flag of the United States of America, and to the Republic for which it stands, one nation under God, indivisible, with liberty and justice for all."
    ~ The U.S. Pledge of Allegiance

During the founding of our country, there was extended debate over the proposed character of our new government. Hamilton and others wanted a strong central or national government, while many, including Jefferson, were wary of too much centralized power and favored stronger state controls. James Madison voiced this concern in Federalist No. 39: *"'But it was not sufficient," say the adversaries of the proposed Constitution, "for the convention to adhere to the republican form. They ought, with equal care, to have preserved the FEDERAL form, which regards the Union as a CONFEDERACY of sovereign states; instead of which, they have framed a NATIONAL government, which regards the Union as a CONSOLIDATION of the States."'*

The debate raged on, and was finally settled with the "Great Compromise," whereby the "national" character was preserved by proportional representation in the House, while the "federal" character was reflected in the equality among states in the Senate, with two senators from each state, elected by state legislators.

While the debate was settled, the skepticism remained. A further attempt to limit the potential for over-reaching by the national government was the statement of enumerated powers of the national legislature defined in Article 1, Section 8 of the Constitution. The 10th Amendment was a further clarification yet of the express and limited nature intended for the government: *"The powers not delegated to the United States by the Constitution, nor prohibited by it to the States, are reserved to the States respectively, or to the people."*

The purpose of all this was to preserve the liberty for which the Revolution was fought; to limit the power of government; to protect against a governing elite; to balance the interests of cities and rural areas and of manufacturing and farming interests; to maintain state and local government and limit that of the national one; and to implement checks and balances within the government to ensure constitutional conformity. *In short, to establish a federal constitutional republic - not a national democracy.* This has all been abused! Somehow, our modern government has missed the point of the critical debate, the great compromise and the Constitution itself.

The alteration of our constitutional republic to this state of affairs has been aided by four major events: the income tax, the 17th Amendment to the Constitution, the Supreme Court decision of Reynolds v. Sims, and the gradual insulation of representatives from the people.

The Income Tax
The present income tax system would have never been approved by the Founders. They might as well have remained under the King. They recognized the need for revenue for the limited and specific needs of government, to be derived from consumption taxes and tariffs. They recognized, that a consumption tax was self-limiting; if it exceeded the willingness of people to give, the people could refuse to spend, thus limiting the tendency of government to consume beyond legitimacy. The income tax gave government absolute power to take to its desires, without restraint. It also conferred the power to discriminate - to favor, to reward, to punish, and to violate basic liberties and personal privacy. It has grown to the abomination we have today.

The solution is to repeal the 16th Amendment, and abolish the income tax and IRS from which they were derived. The replacement would be a single, equal sales tax only system, levied on all goods and services, without discrimination or special favor, collected at the state level and with no other taxes permitted. It would replace the hellish 5.5 million-word tax code with one running perhaps 10-20 pages. It would be naturally progressive, as those who spend more would contribute more, yet all would pay a reasonable share, reflecting the fact that all have an equal voice and vote. It would be a simple extension of the sales tax collection process in place in most states already, and require minimal paperwork. There would be no different rates, no exemption for any individual or organization, no untaxed "underground economy," no invasion of privacy, and no multiple taxation (such as the estate tax and property taxes).

Moreover, it would deny a tyrannical government the ability to use taxes to punish or terrorize, to reward special interests, to manipulate social policy, or to abuse any citizen. It would be transparent as to its increases, instead of being hidden in thousands of different regulations designed for concealing the true cost of government; lowering one visible tax while rising another less so. It would return power to the states as they would collect the revenue and remit to the federal government, reversing the present direction of revenue flow. It would live up the motto of "liberty and justice for all," and reestablish "the republic for which it stands."

The Congress will never willingly consent to such an obvious need; that, after all, is contrary to the self-interest of its members and others from whom they benefit. The Congress will have to be replaced with those who obey the will of the people. It will not be easy; but then neither was the founding from which we were justly empowered to make such change. But it must happen.

17th Amendment
The Constitution provided for the election of representatives by the people, and of the senators by the various state legislatures. In this way, the republican character of the states (assured by the Article 4) would be utilized to encourage a close connection of those representing the states to the states themselves and their residents. It would balance the national/democratic nature of the house with the more federal/republican nature of the Senate. The 17th Amendment was passed by the Congress shortly after the 16th (income tax) Amendment and the two resulted in a fatal transfer of power to a national form of government, impervious to the

people and the states, and acting in its own self-interest at their expense. The stage was set for the consolidation of power, and ultimately, tyranny once again. The abuses of one form of kingdom had simply been replaced by another.

Repeal of the 17th Amendment would return power intended for the states, thereby restoring a measure of republicanism as designed by our Founders. It would return authority and accountability to the states and the interests of people they serve. It will never happen under the current Congress. But it must happen.

Reynolds v. Sims

President Eisenhower remarked that nominating Earl Warren for Chief Justice of the Supreme Court was "the biggest damned-fool mistake I ever made." And Reynolds v. Sims was probably the biggest damned-fool mistake made by Warren. Prior to the case, most state governments, including Nevada, were modeled after the republican form of the federal legislature: one house popularly elected and the other, representing the geographic interests of all, typically by county. Clark County (Las Vegas), for example, with 70% of the state's population would have 70% of the representatives in the Assembly. But each county, regardless of population, would have one state senator. In the same way that the interests of small states were protected in the U.S. Senate, so would the interests of residents outside of Clark County.

Warren, in writing for the majority, advanced his "one man-one vote" position stating that the unequal representation was unfair. In fact, the opposite was true, as can be seen today. A disparate population advantage in one part of a state over others results in the "tyranny of the majority" warned against by de Tocqueville, John Stuart Mill and others. This is one of the major deficiencies of pure democracy! It is one of principle reasons why we were established as a republic.

Warren's foolish logic was wrong then and it is wrong now; it didn't attack unequal representation, it created it. It violates the constitutional requirement to assure each state a republican form of government. It will not be changed by the current Congress, or likely by the current Supreme Court. But it must be changed.

Congress Insulated from the People

At the time of our founding, we were a relatively compact 13 colonies stretching comfortably from Massachusetts to Georgia – about the size of California. The capital in Washington D.C. was equivalent to California's capital in Sacramento - relatively central and accessible to the people.

The nation today ranges from coast to coast, and from Mexico to Canada, and beyond. Washington D.C. is no longer the center of the country, nor are representatives accessible to the people or the people to them. This has given rise to the "Washington Beltway" phenomenon. It has resulted in an insulation of representatives from the people and an undue influence of beltway-based lobbyists representing special interests. Congressmen and Senators no longer live and walk among the people; they are chauffeured among their fellow elite in their own little kingdom – *the Beltway.*

Given the capability of modern telecommunications, there is no need for the Members of Congress to be assembled in Washington D.C. Given the distance from their constituents and the proximity to beltway lobbyists; there is every reason for them not to be. Given the amount of time they are actually doing business on the floor of the Capitol, one wonders why they are there at all.

Members of Congress should be based in the capitals of their home states, within or in the area of their legislatures. Voting and meetings could be conducted electronically and by videoconference. Hearings could be held anywhere in the country, instead of requiring participants to travel to D.C. Members could schedule regular short sessions of attendance in the national capital, say, four times a year or in emergencies as needed. The rest of the time, they would be accessible and visible to the people they serve – not the lobbyists who curry special favor. This will never happen under the current Congress. But it must happen.

The problem with democracy

The essential problem with democracy, and the reason for a republic, is that the former serves the interests of the people as a mob; the latter serves them as a nation of laws.

As James Madison wrote, *"a pure democracy is unwieldy, dangerous in its passion, and subject to mob rule thereby lending itself to instability and violence. Democracies have ever been spectacles of turbulence and contention; have ever been found incompatible with personal security, or the rights of property; and have, in general, been as short in their lives as they have been violent in their deaths."*

Look at some of the "factions," as Madison called them, that our present system serves and what they have gained at the expense of the nation as a whole:

- **Youth** – Irresponsibly lowered the voting age, exempted from military service, and provided "free" college.
- **Hispanics** – Illegal aliens not only tolerated at huge costs to society, but also courted with promises of citizenship.
- **Blacks/Minorities** – $5 trillion in welfare over 50 years with little or no accountability; a transfer of personal responsibility to the state.
- **Environmentalists** – A failed energy system making us reliant on foreign enemies, while failing to utilize our own resources.
- **Unions** – Public employees that work less and earn more than private sector, and have become the largest cost to society with questionable benefit but much red-tape.
- **Big Business** – Tax breaks, subsidies, and grants to the biggest and often least efficient or effective (look at Freddie Mac and Fanny Mae).
- **Homosexuals** – Marriages that defy nature, culture, and common sense.

If this weren't bad enough, foreign nations have joined the bandwagon receiving military protection, economic aid, and trade deals that damage our own economy, and benefits not even available to U.S. citizens.

The most egregious faction of all is, of course, the Congress itself. Members are inclined to support other special interests to justify their generosity to themselves in pay, pensions, medical care, special perks, lifetime "employment", travel, and more. Not to mention the insider abuses: million-dollar land deals and billion-dollar contracts awarded to family and friends.

This will never change under the current Congress. But it must change.

"If we resort for a criterion to the different principles on which different forms of government are established, we may define a republic to be, or at least may bestow that name on, a government which derives all its powers directly or indirectly from the great body of the people, and is administered by persons holding their offices during pleasure, for a limited period, or during good behavior. It is ESSENTIAL to such a government that it be derived from the great body of the society, not from an inconsiderable proportion, or a favored class of it; otherwise a handful of tyrannical nobles, exercising their oppressions by a delegation of their powers, might aspire to the rank of republicans, and claim for their government the honorable title of republic."
– Federalist No. 39, James Madison

§

THE NANNY NATION (MAR 2006)

"Government exists to protect us from each other. Where government has gone beyond its limits is in deciding to protect us from ourselves."
   ~ Ronald Reagan

In the aftermath of the Katrina hurricane that devastated New Orleans, two things are striking: the need to place blame (especially in the wrong places) and the desire to spend recklessly. Contrast this to the early American pioneers. Consider the Donner Party in particular. After all, the federal government – and George Bush *especially* – HAD to have known that a snowstorm was coming. The Donner folks should have been warned and FEMA should have airlifted supplies, fresh horses, and mobile homes to last out the winter. Never mind that these folks set out of their own volition, knew the risks, and took their chances.

But the Donner party didn't blame George Bush – or even the government. They didn't expect counseling from the life altering effects of canni-balism. They didn't even ask for burial costs and replacement of their wagons. Back then, there was something called "personal choice" and it was accompanied by "personal responsibility." It was very much an American tradition. Coupled with freedom, democracy, and limited government, those concepts shaped a nation – the greatest the world has known. *A Nanny Nation is taking its place.*

The Nanny Nation is a place where no one is ever wrong or responsible for their choices or actions, except for invisible enemies: the government (Conservative administrations only), big business, and white, European males. In the Nanny Nation, everyone (except white, European males) is entitled to compensation for most anything that adversely affects their lives – and the compensation is paid by someone else (mostly, white European males). There are no accidents or tragedies in the Nanny nation. After all, without blame, there is no one from whom to siphon money.

In Nannyland, you are freed from the burden of personal choice – the government, or one of its favored special interest groups, will make choices for you. You may try to make your own choices, but they will be ostracized, taxed, inconvenienced, or made illegal.

Life is good in the Nanny State. There is free entertainment, free education, free meals, free medical care and prescription drugs, free housing, and more – especially nice is the free choice without responsibility.

In fact, in the world of Nanny thinking, even behaviors considered "bad" are encouraged. After all, it's not your fault. Strict upbringing, race, immigration status, economic status, language limitations, sex, or some other external influence MADE you the way you are. You can't be expected to have control over your life, and therefore can't be held responsible. If you get pregnant, don't know the father, and don't work, Nanny will take care of you: free prenatal care, free delivery, free formula, and free diapers. Nanny will make your child breakfast, lunch and dinner, and provide free day care for your little state-programmed automaton while you pursue your degree in "Welfare Services," "Multi-cultural Studies" or "Feminism and Angry White Males."

If you pop out your 10th illegitimate child, Nanny considers it sort of a lottery win, and you will be expected to stay home to care for your future drug users and criminals, and you will be paid hundreds or even thousands of dollars in monthly stipends for your heroic accomplishment.

If you are a drug user, you will be given free needles to ensure they are clean – after all, contaminated drugs are dangerous! You will get Nanny paid counseling to assist you in getting off of the nasty drugs but don't worry – it's not your fault. You are ill, and in the Nanny Nation, no one who is ill is punished.

Well, no one except those awful, awful smokers and drinkers. If you smoke, drink, or eat red meat you are simply bad. After all, these are legal activities, paid for by you, and for which you take personal responsibility. Nothing could be less Nanny-like and you will have to be punished.

You will be taxed and treated like the criminal that you are. You will be scrutinized especially carefully even if you do nothing wrong except have evidence of the contraband products in your system. If you smoke at home, you may be fired (drug use is OK – Nanny says you're ill and need treatment). If you own a gun, you are very likely to be considered among the worst of liberty seekers – those who persist in the silly notion that control may ever be taken away from Nanny.

Nanny used to be described as the "welfare state" but that was far too limiting. Why stop at "cradle to grave" free stuff when you can control choices *before* birth and *after* death. Look at the victims of 9/11. They were not simply in the wrong place at the wrong time – they were Nanny-approved "victims." And unlike the unknown thousands who die on our roads every year and receive nothing, catastrophe victims are a special class: *they are visible!* As such, 9/11 families got a $7 billion gift from Nanny – an average of $2.1 million per "victim" plus another $400,000 for injuries.

The Katrina "victims" were also dealt a bad hand that the Nanny Nation will fix. After all, who would have guessed that a city 8-feet below sea level would ever flood? Who could have seen that awful hurricane coming in an age of long-range weather forecasting, 24-hour news, and televisions in even the poorest of households? Besides, what if you were too poor to have a car, and Nanny hadn't gotten free transportation to you yet? What if you had no bicycle? No skateboard? Limited physical abilities? Well, now we cross the line from Nannyspeak to compassion. You see, if you haven't the *ability* to leave a pending disaster, compassionate people will help you. But if you simply haven't got the brains to move away from a hurricane, Nanny still won't hold you responsible. All things considered, it really is George Bush's fault – *and* white, European males. As a consequence of such thinking, Katrina "victims" will receive about $200 billion, or $400,000 for every displaced family. The 1906 San Francisco quake was probably more devastating and people rebounded with little federal help – *but Nanny wasn't around then.*

Nanny Nation is not bound by rules; it will invent its own as it goes along to make sure the right things are done. How do we know the right things? Simple – whatever Nanny wants is the right thing. You have no choices; you don't need them – Nanny takes care of you. Nanny made 30 million people obese overnight by changing the definition of obese. Michael Jordan is now overweight – so are Tom Cruise and Arnold Schwarzenegger. Now with so many fat people, Nanny can tax fast food, remove soft drinks from schools, and encourage lawsuits against un-Nannylike organizations such as McDonalds.

In the world of Nanny, no one's feelings are hurt (except of course, white European males). It is necessary to put all cultures and views on an equal footing – even though "99%" of all advances in history were created by white European males. So we will not have "White European Male" Month. We will have Black History Month. Remember, whatever Nanny says is right, *is* right. We will also have Black and Hispanic Chambers of Commerce. Oh yes, and a Gay Olympics. "But," you say, "don't we live in a color-blind society?" Silly person - Nanny is right – you must remember that.

Now, if you want to brainstorm this matter more, I'm sorry but you will have either "word storm" or "thought shower." You see, those without brains – or those who fail to use them – could be offended. And that is just not acceptable in the Nanny Nation.

§

INCREMENTALISM (JAN 2003)

"I believe there are more instances of the abridgement of freedom of the people by gradual and silent encroachments by those in power than by violent and sudden usurpations."
        ~ James Madison

The politics of incrementalism are exemplified in three issues that have received, and will continue to receive, a great deal of discussion: taxes, homosexuality and racial preference. Incremental change is based on the popular analogy of the frog in the pot. Place a frog in a pot of boiling water and it will realize the danger immediately and jump out. But, place a frog in a pot of cool water and incrementally turn up the heat and the frog will gradually adjust and relax until it is cooked. There are two common forms of incremental change: multi-faceted and multi-layered.

• **Multi-faceted incrementalism:** The payroll tax started out at a 2% in 1935 and applied to the first $3,000 of income. It grew to 6% in 1960 and 12.4% in 2000. the income threashold also steadily grew to $76,200 in 2000. In addition, the age for collection of benefits has steadily been increased and additional gimmicks, such as offsetting against other income have been employed. This is incremental sleight of hand at its finest.

• **Multi-layered incrementalism:** If it works with one tax, why not apply to a myriad of them - and government does. We have taxes and fees on virtually every aspect of life: taxes on productivity; taxes on "sin;" taxes on living and taxes on dying; taxes on people, payrolls and equipment. Virtually all of them started off small, and were incrementalized up to higher and higher levels.

The income tax started out as a 1% on the millionaires of the time. A cap of 10% was discussed, but rejected as preposterous. It could not be imagined that income would ever be taxed above 10%. They underestimated the elite's appetite for the power of money. Rates over the past 90 years have ranged from onerous to obscene, and the games played with exemptions, exclusions, withholdings, transfers, and more have hidden the travesty of the scheme to many. Still, the incremental approach is being used effectively by those who will gladly take all you have, to support their own arrogant agenda. *After all, they know better than you do.*

Homosexual incrementalism has been well on its way for some time. Homosexuality in modern times has generally been treated as a personal, private matter, as has sexuality in general. Emboldened by legitimate "civil rights" issues of the 1960s, homosexuals began a public campaign initially for *tolerance* of their private lifestyle; to be treated as any other individual. They got that, and reasonably so. That grew to *acceptance* of homosexual behavior as an alternative private lifestyle. Then public displays in "Gay Pride" parades and open homosexual acts in clubs and bathhouses. Then acceptance of public behavior in the workplace, the classroom, and entertainment venues. The values, beliefs, and choices of anyone else were not to be considered, only those of the homosexual.

The mainstream issue has now incrementalized to forced acceptance of homosexual marriage, a blatant conflict with long established societal values and traditions. Clearly, the homosexual agenda goal is for *absolute normalization* of an inherently abnormal lifestyle. While the vast majority of Americans feel little or no animosity toward homosexuals, and are tolerant of private sexual rights between consenting adults, they still reject the lifestyle as abnormal, unnatural and, for many, immoral. But those opinions are marginalized by the educational establishment, mainstream media, and many in the courts and politics. *Traditional values and attitudes have been incrementalized into insignificance.*

The Supreme Court issued a ruling in a Texas sodomy case ruling *not* based on homosexual tolerance, but on personal privacy rights within the home. In this context, the ruling was fair and proper. No reasonable person wants the govrenment snooping into people's bedrooms or into matters of personal privacy between consenting adults. True, there are moral issues which may be undermined – but the essential line has to be drawn at public versus private behavior in such matters. The values, morals, and beliefs of the majority of Americans will continue to be tested – incrementally. They better be prepared and resolved to deal with it.

The issue of racial preferences was also dealt with by the Supreme Court, which to some degree, rolled back the long history of incrementalism in this area. The Court granted that race may reasonably be considered as a factor at the University of Michigan Law School, but flatly rejected the firm and excessive 20% admissions bonus based simply on race and ethnicity (well, some races and some ethnicities). It is somewhat heartening that the court finally said there are limits. After 50 years of preferences of one sort or another, despite special accomodations and wholesale demolition of barriers to the advance of *any* individual based on achievement, the time has come to end all racial preference. We would like to see true equality of opportunity, elevated to its proper constitutional place. It appears that we will have to wait for another day. But at least the incremental policies in this area were held in check.

So how do incremental politics get started in the first place? How are they allowed to progress? The answer is simple – *we let them*. One small step at a time. Just like the frog in the pot.

§

IS GOVERNMENT MORAL? (APR 2008)

"The purpose of government is to enable the people of a nation to live in safety and happiness. Government exists for the interests of the governed, not for the governors."
~ Thomas Jefferson

Is government moral? No, it is not; *nor should it be.* When it presumes to be, results of its actions are usually themselves immoral. It is a mistake to think of institutions as having either moral duties, or a capacity for moral behavior. A corporation is not moral; neither is a country. The only duty of the corporation is to serve its long-term interests by producing products or providing services that create profits and provide an optimal return to its shareholders. The only duty of our government is to the people of this country as defined by their Constitution. All other duties are fictions; the creations of devious minds to achieve some purpose of self-interest, or to impose a duty which is not theirs to impose.

The objective of moral behavior by government has no legitimate basis. Nowhere in the Constitution is there a prerequisite for moral behavior by the government; in fact the word "moral" is not to be found. There is a provision punishing Members of Congress for disorderly behavior. There is a requirement that judges "hold their offices during periods of good behavior." There are also references to individual behaviors that may be characterized in moral terms, such as treason, bribery, "high crimes and misdemeanors." All of these moral issues pertain to *people*; there is no reference to a collective morality of the government. The proper behavior of the government is only to do, or not do, specific things; and they are invariably *not* based on moral assumptions.

The functions of government that ARE specified in the Constitution are explicit, and include the following:

• To protect the country from attack or invasion, secure its borders and declare war.

• To maintain domestic tranquility.
• To lay and collect uniform taxes for the common defense and general welfare of the nation.
• To borrow money, regulate foreign commerce and enter into treaties, appoint ambassadors or key government officials, including judges.

The proper role of government is neither moral nor immoral. It is properly *amoral*. That is, it is not concerned with moral judgments - only constitutional duties. So why does all this matter? After all, we are generally a moral nation of people; and morality exists at the level of the individual. It matters because the goal of moral behavior by government is foolish, costly, and dangerous, at best. And in the worst cases, it promotes tyranny by justifying unconstitutional authority based on a perceived moral right or duty. Some applications ~

War
War is about protecting our country from attack, and responding to attackers or preempting likely potential attacks. It is about killing those who would kill us, destroying their military capacity and destroying their national infrastructure. War is immoral when the individuals who wage it do so without justification. Once government declares war, it is conducted on constitutional authority and military principles, not perceived moral duties.

We have undermined our capacity for war (and therefore the defense and safety of our country, our military forces, and our citizens) by assuming a moral stance by government instead of one that performs the duties of defense and the conduct of war objectively and without emotion. American lives have been lost as a result, with more likely to follow.

In Iraq, we have wrongly concluded that it is our moral duty to train the military of the new government, to build schools and hospitals, and to make safe their cities and borders. That is pure nonsense. If we had any reason to go into Iraq and Afghanistan, it was preemption against terrorist activities that might have included chemical, biological, and nuclear threats; it was to protect the U.S. interests in oil being produced in the Middle East; and it was retaliation to the unprovoked attack of 9/11 in which 3,000 civilians were killed. Once those objectives were met, we should have withdrawn. It is the misperception of a governmental moral duty that is keeping us there.

Domestic Spending

You have two neighbors. One is hard working, frugal, and productive and lives quite comfortably, taking care of his family's needs and wants. The other is a lazy spendthrift, uneducated by choice, unemployed, and living beyond his means while neglecting the needs of his family. Is it government's moral duty to take from the one neighbor and give to the other? Does it have a moral right to do so? "NO" – but our government believes so. Not only does government engage in behavior that is beyond its constitutional duties and powers, it does so based on an improper sense of morality

Government is *amoral*. With few exceptions, it has neither a right nor a duty to make one life better at the expense of another.

Government takes on all manner of such illegitimate roles, taking money from one person and giving it to another, under the guise of a moral duty that it does not have:
• Free public education
• College grants
• Health care insurance and expense payments
• Meals at school
• Pre-school (baby sitting)
• Recreation
• Unemployment payments and welfare
• Research and other grants
• Farm and other subsidies
• Bailouts of private corporations and homeowner with loans they can't support
• Katrina-type assistance to those who can't understand not to build or live below sea level, on cliffs or in other high hazard areas

The list could go on *ad infinitum*, including the bureaucracies needed to support these functions, none of which are constitutionally mandated! Government spends almost $3 trillion annually at the federal level and another $600 billion by the states. Most of the spending has nothing to do with the legitimate functions of government, but instead is based on a tortured sense of moral right or obligation.

Public education is an example of the slippery slope of government morality. The argument is that society benefits when its citizens are educated. There is truth to this, but there are any number of benefits to the individual that extend to society, and are not paid for by the public. Why education? Moreover, there is a direct correlation between cost and value. When there is no cost, there is little responsibility to use something wisely and judiciously. Kids are not motivated, and many families fail to insist on educational performance, because it costs them nothing. Neither is there much demand for the educational establishment to contain costs because someone else pays! If each child in school required a co-payment of some reasonable percentage of the cost of education, students would perform better, parents would be more involved, and there would be parental and community pressure to keep educational costs in line with true needs – not ever-growing wants.

Between free education, free health care (SCHIP program), and free meals at school, there is little incentive to restrict family size to afford-ability. Hillary Clinton proposed a "wonderful" way to ensure that those who can least afford them will have more kids – give them a $5,000 bonus at birth. What an incentive! All of these benefits, of course, are provided by taking money from one segment of society and giving it to another – *immorally*.

International Aid
Our government has no constitutional duty to fund the needs of other nations. Not for military support, not for food, not for disease, nor for any other purpose. The only justifiable reason for aiding other countries is for mutual benefit in alliances, treaties, or trade agreements. The key

is "mutual benefit." To the extent even loans are made, we must insist on repayment with interest – we expect no less of citizens; why should countries be given a free ride. They possess the rights and duties of sovereign status. We owe them nothing, except that which may be to our benefit, as defined in treaties and agreements.

Thinking of government as having moral duties to other nations opens an incredible "can of worms." If we are obligated to feed one nation, why not all. If we are to cure the diseases of one nation, why not all. If we are to build the infrastructure for one nation's benefit, why not all. Our duties lie only within our borders and within the constraints of our Constitution unless there is a quid pro quo that is beneficial to us as a whole.

Trampling the Rights of Citizens
Taking property from an individual outside the provisions of the Constitution is wrong, no matter how moral the action might appear to those supporting it. The rights of citizens are enshrined in our Constitution, not the right of government to act in ways it considers good, useful or moral without a constitutional provision to do so. Except for its limited and defined responsibilities, government has no right to take your property, your money, your thoughts or beliefs, or any other aspect of your being. It may not tell you what to do with your money or your property, limit your choices of association, or dictate what you must think or believe.

When government institutes behavioral standards, by requirement or incentive, it is making moral choices not its right or purpose to make. Racial quotas, income preferences, age preferences, and similar such standards are not the proper role of government. They typically involve moral outcomes desired by those in favor, while infringing on others. Life, liberty, and the pursuit of happiness are constitutionally protected rights; specified outcomes are not.

The Most Immoral Tax
The income tax is the primary weapon by which government wages war against the rights of citizens and takes on its moral imperatives. It

provides unlimited ability to take, giving it unlimited ability to define needs that it perceives as morally right. It takes unequally because it asserts a moral right to do so. In fact, an uneven playing field only exists because some people work harder, get better educated, take more risks, or otherwise earn what is theirs. Our government undermines that with redistribution from some to others for one "moral" purpose or other. An income tax is a tax on success and is often used to reward failure. It is not limited to funding the legitimate needs of government but for all manner of social engineering to achieve desired outcomes. Families who have children they can't afford are rewarded. Those who fail to educate themselves are propped up. People who work for their personal needs only are elevated to equal standing with those who excel, risk, invest, and create opportunity.

Many other taxes are invented for the sole purpose of penalizing one element of society and rewarding another. Surveys that demonstrate a willingness to tax invariably reflect a tax on someone else. Taxing Peter to pay Paul is, after all, always supported by Paul.

The only way to limit the excess and abuse of funding for government is to limit its ability to take. As long as the government has the unlimited ability to tax, it has the unlimited ability to expand its scope beyond legitimacy.

Individual Moral Behavior

Humanitarianism is an individual trait, not a government one. If individuals desires to spend their own money or contribute their time, property or effort to a cause they deem worthy, that is their right. Such actions are noble because they reflect personal choice, not government fiat. If Bill Gates wants to give a billion dollars for AIDS prevention in Africa, that is his choice. If, however, our government takes *one dollar* from its citizens to do so, it is morally wrong. Such an action is justified as moral, but it is not. It takes from citizens against their will for purposes not constitutionally justified.

Government, like other organizations, can facilitate the humanitarian desires of its citizens by serving as a conduit for voluntary aid; for the flow of money and the distribution of goods as directed. It cannot rightfully presume to determine from whom that aid should come, or to whom it should be directed.

An individual who acts morally is virtuous; a government that attempts to do so is wrong at best, and tyrannical in the worst cases. Our government has taken on the behavior of the latter; and is bankrupting both our nation and its people in doing so. Yet, while the financial malfeasance is an incredible burden, it is the permanent damage to our liberty that is most intolerable.

"I cannot undertake to lay my finger on that article of the Constitution which granted a right to Congress of expending, on objects of benevolence, the money of their constituents..." --James Madison

§

SOVEREIGNTY UNDER ATTACK (JAN 2004)

"A state can no more give up part of her sovereignty than a lady can give up part of her virtue"
  ~ John Randolph

The concept of sovereignty has become unfamiliar to our citizens; almost quaint. And yet it is sovereignty that defines our status as a nation. Our constitutional rights and duties were made possible by the sovereignty established in our break from England 230 years ago. *Today, our sovereignty hangs by a thread.*

Sovereignty is that recognition of a nation as free and independent, with the sole right to govern affairs within its borders and with final responsibility to and authority over the citizens from whom it derives its existence.

There are two primary attacks on our sovereignty: an external and directly dangerous attack together with a more insidious, internal one. The external attack is via the United Nations and other organizations and programs supported by Internationalists and "New World Order" types. The internal attack is through a dilution of our culture and our language encouraged by Multi-culturalists, and a direct assault on our institutions, our economy and our way of life through the intentional violation of our borders by illegal immigrants. *How do we protect our nation's sovereignty against these threats?*

The agenda of the United Nations and much of its membership, is not supportive of the United States – it is, in fact, antagonistic towards it. The reasons are many, but the message is clear: the U.N. has become a bloated international bureaucracy with far more influence than is justified, much of it exercised by petty tyrants and ego rich international celebrities. The actions in Afghanistan and Iraq are but the latest in a long history of U.N. failures detrimental to the interests of the U.S. and its true allies. It is time to replace it.

There is merit in the idea that the international community needs an organized body to assist in the progress towards world peace, encourage the development of poorer nations, and facilitate relations on the world stage. The inclusion of rogue, terror sponsoring and tyrant run states is counterproductive however. While there is room for a diversity of culture, there needs to be a commonality too: religion and economic systems, a fundamental commitment to human rights, some form of democratic system, and a national demeanor of peacefulness. Not all of the world's nations should be allowed to participate; in fact, many would be purposely excluded unless, and until, they mended their ways. It is through international stigma, economic limitations, and a united force among those opposing them that such nations might likely effect change. Unlike the United Nations, the mission of such a replacement body would need to be clearly stated, expressly limited, and funded proportionally by all the member nations. The functions would be limited to: global peace, fair trade, stability, and sound environmental practices.

A separate organization, a replacement for NATO and other military alliances, would be created to address the express issue of uniform military stance for the protection of member nations, and those living peaceably among them. It would be a more limited body, based on military capacity and a common set of values, the preservation of which would be the common goal. While such a body might include long-standing allies such as Australia, England, France and Germany, the ability to act would not require unanimity, and might more closely resemble the coalition assembled by President Bush in the war on Iraq. Free from the bureaucratic nature of the U.N., it would likely function more responsively and be less politically driven. Such a capacity would result in swift and sure reaction, retribution and retaliation when justified, including preemptive measures as may be occasioned by severe and supportable threats to world peace, or that of any member nation. This would be a "no-nonsense" coalition of the "peaceful but powerful," and no rogue nation on earth would test its resolve without immediate and severe consequences.

The era of years and years of threats, resolutions, and saber rattling would be gone, and those perpetrating evil would be dispatched quickly and permanently. The threat posed by a nuclear N. Korea and Iran would be immediately addressed by a pre-emtive force of western, democratic nations exerting a joint military response, once and for all. There would be no blaming of the U.S. for acting alone; no phoney protection under a Russian or Chinese umbrella; and no foot dragging while the threat continued to full nuclear capacity. The lesson to the next rogue nation would be unambiguously clear.

While the threat to our sovereignty from without is clear and simple, the internal threat is more complex and insidious. There are estimates of 12-20 million illegal residents in our country today – many feel the true number may be much higher. Half or more of these trespassers are from Mexico which, therefore, must be the primary focus. The justifications for tolerating such an assault on our borders are many. None have a legitimate foundation, and all ignore the serious consequences in the loss of our nation's sovereignty.

There are justifiable reasons for encouraging legal visitation, residence and application for citizenship to our country. Certainly, the visitation by those from other nations is to be encouraged for social, family, cultural, economic, tourist, and other legitimate reasons. The desire for foreigners to seek employment and receive the benefits of that employment affect many industries and also needs to be reasonably accommodated. Lastly, our country has a long and noble history of welcoming immigrants. America's strength lies in the diversity of its citizenry woven into a single, assimilated fabric reflecting American traditions and a unique cultural uniformity.

The problem with illegal – as contrasted to legal – immigration, is that its agenda is wholly different from, and often antagonistic to the assimilation process. Some come here illegally to cause direct harm to the United States and its citizens, as we know all too well. Many others come here simply to take, and not to embrace the full range of both rights and responsibilities of being an American. They want to *be* in America, but not be an *American*.

Their allegiance is to a foreign land, a condition that is corrosive to the values and culture of America. Others still, come with disease, criminal backgrounds, or other liabilities. Many come simply for the benefits of social programs for themselves, their families, and their offspring to come, thereby draining the taxpayers of this country, with little given in return.

A proper program of immigration would address the legitimate needs and responsibilities of our nation, while vigorously defending it against attack by illegal entry. Components of such a program would include the following:

1.   The proper characterization and recognition of entry as either legal or illegal – *period*.

2.   Procedures for visitation that vary depending on the background of the individual and his country of origin. Proper credentials, visitation purpose, and travel between countries with normal and peaceful relations would be stream-lined and require minimal interference. Visits from countries, or by individuals, with suspect backgrounds or motives, or strained military or diplomatic relation-ships, might require fingerprinting, photographing, detention and interviewing, and other more aggressive measures prior to entry. Cooperation from the origi-nating country would be a requirement; failure to establish cooperative policies might move that country to a less welcome status. Finally, countries with which we have severe differences, for example, those sponsoring terrorism, would be banned, except for the most stringent and necessary purposes, and only under the most demanding and rigorous entry provisions. Such a ban would apply to student visas as well; *there is no intelligent reason for educating the citizens of countries dedicated to the destruction of the United States.*

3.   A program similar to that for visitation would be developed for longer term or permanent residency. Such residency would be granted only when a clear mutual benefit is established between the visitor and this country based on skills, education, financial capacity, and a moral and law-abiding character. The characteristics of those seeking permanent residence would be quite similar to those for naturalization and citizenship, the end goal being the primary difference.

4. A program for temporary employment in critical industries such as agriculture, hospitality, and other high demand/low supply jobs would be established. Such a program, unlike current programs, would have a high degree of control and cooperation between our government, our employers, and the legally resident temporary workers. Limits would be placed on the period of residence (short term), identification and regular reporting would be required to ensure compliance, and participation would be limited to adult males and non-pregnant females. A regular medical exam, employer provided, would be required of females, and pregnancy would be grounds for termination and return to country of residence. Close and complete cooperation of the host countries would be a condition for the program, and host countries would be expected to prosecute or support prosecution of violators.

5. A change in our method of taxation to ensure that all visitors, workers, and immigrants would pay their fair share of taxes since taxation would be based on consumption, not income and other complex forms of taxation.

6. All illegal entrants would be prosecuted when caught, as would those facilitating illegal entry. Conviction of illegal would bar an individual from participating in any legal entry visitation or worker program for 5 years; double conviction would bar permanently any entry as well as application for citizenship. A treaty between host countries would be required to enforce the provisions of prosecution and conviction. The host country, not America, would be responsible for the costs of criminal sanctions, such as incarceration.

7. Our borders would be permanently protected and sealed with a combination of roving border patrols, the establishment of military bases at frequent intervals along our borders, and the use of technology such as laser detection, satellite surveillance, and other means to ensure detection and apprehension of illegal entrants.

8. A constitutional amendment would require that citizenship by birth would be limited to individuals born to parents, at least one of whom is a U.S. citizen and the other is either a citizen or a legal resident.

9. Much more stringent standards would be developed and mandated for citizenship, attendance in U.S. schools, or for utilization of other taxpayer provided services, such as health care and social services. English speaking would be a requirement and all public documents would be available only in English. To accommodate such a requirement, states would be encouraged to implement reasonable cost programs for immersion instruction in English so that reasonable fluency could be expected in a one-year program of instruction.

We do not support any mechanism that would grant automatic legal status to those who have entered illegally. We do not support a program for immigration that does not address ALL the issues of border security, cultural integrity, and safety. We believe that the intolerable condition of illegal occupation in this country needs to be addressed before *any* program for accommodation of immigrants is considered. A moratorium on immigration should be implemented while the matter is analyzed and a comprehensive long-term solution is enacted. Any other such approach should be vigorously protested.

The United States is among the most free, generous, and peaceful nations on earth. It is unquestionably the most powerful and economically successful. It is time for it to exercise its prerogatives in re-establishing a system of world organizations that work, while preserving the sovereignty of all nations. The United States is a nation of immigrants who have historically been welcome as long as they arrive legally, assume both the rights and responsibilities of citizenship, and assimilate into a culture long established. It is time for it to assert reasonable demands for visitors, residents, and new citizens to comply with legitimate requirements; to welcome those who do, and to reject and prosecute those who don't. The continued sovereignty of a great nation hangs in the balance.

§

CHAPTER 4

FAILED SYSTEMS
Political

"However [political parties] may now and then answer popular ends, they are likely in the course of time and things, to become potent engines, by which cunning, ambitious, and unprincipled men will be enabled to subvert the power of the people and to usurp for themselves the reins of government, destroying afterwards the very engines which have lifted them to unjust dominion."
     ~ George Washington,
     Farewell Address, Sep. 17, 1796

THE ONE PARTY SYSTEM (NOV 2003)

Meet the new Republicans: *Democrats*. Meet the new Democrats: *Republicans*. Together, the two groups form the new one party system: the *RepubliCrats*.

There was a time, arguably some decades ago, when the two major political parties had distinctly different ideas about how to govern, the nature and extent of government, and the goals for society as a whole. Candidates came from many walks of life, served if elected and then, after a modest period of public service, went home to the life they held before and outside politics. True, politics even then required a certain spirit of compromise, but there were fundamental principles that defined each party that were not subject to negotiation. Come to think of it, there were principles that defined most *politicians* that were not subject to negotiation or compromise.

The climate of politics has changed. In recent years, Democrats have become split into two camps. Those on the left have gone ever so far left that they are hardly distinguishable from Socialists. Among these is their "spiritual" leader, Hillary Clinton, along with Nancy Pelosi, Chuck Schumer, Harry Reid, Barbara Boxer, most of the black Democratic caucus, Ted Kennedy, Barney Frank, and other ideologues of the far left. They love the State; they love nationalizing everything. There is not a need that can be imagined that national government cannot and should not get its hands on: erecting new agencies, passing new regulations, and collecting more and more money to fund the liberal agenda. They willingly enslave the masses in exchange for more government care and protection. They believe government knows better than the citizens themselves what is best for them. National medical care, national welfare, and national public education are hallmarks of their agenda and tools of change, ensnaring all those who accept the Faustian bargain of big government.

The Constitution is merely an historic guide to such people, to be redefined by liberal, activist courts. The language and culture of America is an anachronism, which needs refinement by Internationalists, Multiculturalists, and Progressives. Rights are trumpeted while duties are ignored; except for the primary allegiance to government as supreme.

Joining this socialist left agenda are most of America's academics, including the education establishment down to primary grades. Also included are the mainstream press, headed by the far left NY Times, Washington Post, and network television. Support is automatic from the social welfare establishment, inventing needs even where none exist. The Hollywood elite and pop-culture icons are solidly in this camp. Fame and money come far too easily, thus riddling them with guilt and a need to spend someone *else's* money for *their* worthy causes.

Though bankrupt of new ideas, this group is dangerous. They occupy and wield much power in the political arena and dictate their ideological version of government to young minds; they steer the perspective of the masses with headline journalism; and they poison traditional culture through "entertainment." They continue to occupy power through a time-honored technique of dividing Americans into special interest groups, tossing goodies to each faction to endear and enslave. The far left Democrats have effectively devolved, from a legitimate political party to a pandering, leftist ideology; their interests are not those of the the nation, but instead, their own narrow, self-serving agenda - the nation be damned.

On the far right, there are extremists too, though these individuals and groups have lessened influence as the mainstream media, education, and pop-culture establishments have effectively branded them as kooks, radicals, and extremists. No such characterizations exist, of course, on the left, though one can argue that they are actually the larger and more dangerous group of extremists. The effectiveness in marginalizing the extreme right is so good that many non-extremists are incorporated into it. Thus, anyone professing Christian beliefs is suspect, as is anyone suggesting a debate on abortion. The same is true for advocates of the 2nd Amendment or even the Constitution as a whole. They simply cannot be trusted, according to the Left, including the Secretary of Homeland Security! Clearly, the very far right who advocate violence, white supremacy, and anarchy are not part of mainstream conservatism, though the media loves to imply so.

So what remains of the traditional political parties? Well, the bulk of those occupying power are comprised of the *RepubliCrats*. These are the more moderate Democrats, and the leftward drifting Republicans. The former have recognized the need to moderate their views for elect-ability – they can be whatever you need them to be to get elected, but if they have the votes, they will turn far left at the drop of a hat. Ironically, they have been joined by a block of Republicans that also yield principle to expediency. Increasingly, they are willing to sacrifice principles such as smaller government, lower taxes, allegiance to our Constitution, and preservation of our culture for the sake of votes. What combines these two strange bedfellows is a loyalty to their self-interest. As long as they can get elected, and stay in office, they will do whatever it takes. In the process, they will vote themselves more benefits, more pay, and more advantages to keep challengers at bay. They will pander and gerrymander, cave to special interests, and throw America and Americans to the wolves – *so long as they can stay in power.* The two groups have melded into a one party system where self-interest reigns supreme.

There is hope in resurrecting a true second party (or creating a third) which represents the will of the people and traditional American values, respects the Constitution, and puts principle above permanent self-interest. To do this requires coalescing those citizens left out of the cozy RepubliCrat arrangement, who support neither the Socialist Left or the Radical Right. This group is comprised of traditional Republicans, Libertarians, and Independents. The last of these has been disaffected by party politics and jaded to the point of non-participation, but they tend to fall philosophically into the center-right orientation typical of most Americans.

Some issues need to be resolved not by compromise, but by reason. Republicans need to back away from some hard-core stances on personal matters that are not the function of government to dictate, and Libertarians have to accept that a civil society requires some limits on personal choice. The independents simply have to be convinced to put aside their cynicism and join the party. Out of reason, justice, and common sense, a new alliance can be forged and a new party born. It's time to "baptize" this baby and get started! As to what it should be called? How about "The Party Formerly Know As Republicans."

"I would rather live in a society governed by the first 2,000 names in the Boston phone directory than in one governed by the 2,000 members of the Harvard faculty."
~ *William F. Buckley*

§

IF CONGRESSMEN LIVED LIKE US (FEB 2008)

"It could probably be shown by facts and figures that there is no distinctly native American criminal class except Congress."
  ~ Mark Twain

In November of 2004, 401 of the 435 sitting members of the U.S. House of Representatives sought reelection. Of those, all but five were reelected. There must be a reason (a) why they didn't leave, or (b) why citizens returned them to office. The second part has more to do with the stranglehold the major parties and incumbents have on the political process. But the first part is simple: *life in political office is good – very good.*

But what if Members of Congress had to live like the rest of us?

Base Pay
As of January 2008, the Members of the House and Senate get paid $169,300 per year. Senator Majority Leader Reid gets $188,100 while House Speaker Nancy Pelosi gets $217,400. Heck, the president only makes $400,000.

Pretty good money considering the bang-up job Congress has been doing over the past 50 years. As good as it is it seems, it is not much considering the millions they spend to get elected. Of course, the fact that they get elected with *your* money - not theirs - is part of the reason. But there must be more to the equation. *There is.*

Lawmakers also receive an annual adjustment in pay equal to the change in the government's Employment Cost Index. This increase – thanks to recent legislation – takes place *automatically*, unless the Members specifically vote against it. Pretty slick.

Now if they were like the rest of us, they would get paid the median income for the state they represent. For Nevada, they would make $50,819 and from high priced and high tax New Jersey they would earn a whopping $64,169. Oh yes, and no automatic pay raises. They would get increases like the rest of us ...as determined by their "employer"... and only if the performance of the "company" justified it.

Family Help
It's hard to make ends meet on $170,000 so the Members get creative. At least 19 Members have spouses on their staff, earning a reported total of $637,000 from 2005- 2007. Of course, this may not be taxpayer money; it likely comes from campaign contributions. There are more than a few politician's kids and spouses employed by lobbyists too. No conflict there - perfectly legal. If they were like the rest of us, the spouses and kids would have to go get a job outside those funded by special interests; maybe working in a bank, a store, or teaching school - just like regular folks.

Benefits
Public employees get the best benefits of any employment sector. They are not like us. Members of Congress make out even better. Congress likes to compare their work to that of senior public executives, so they treat them very well. They don't like to compare themselves to small entrepreneurs – the ones who create all the jobs and most of the wealth – so they treat them poorly. *It's good to be King.*

Health Care
Members get free outpatient medical care at Bethesda Naval Hospital and Walter Reed Army Medical Center, while thousands of veterans are denied access to military or VA hospitals. Members get taxpayer subsidized health insurance; very comprehensive plans, not the ones you and I get. They utilize the "Office of the Attending Physician" - on site treatment in the Capitol complex – for $275/year for House Members and $520/year for Senators. *It costs you that much for few office visits.* They will exempt themselves from inclusion in a proposed government database of medical records, or any other health care "reform" – *count on it.*

I suggest they live like we do. Go to the doctor and take a number. Fill out a bunch of forms, hope your insurance covers some of the cost (assuming you have insurance), and pray you don't need to go to the hospital. Better have a check or credit card – payment may be due at the time of treatment. Access to health care treatment and insurance should be the same as any average individual or self-employed small businessperson. Then they would know what the real world of health care is like.

Travel

Do you think Barbara Boxer takes off her shoes, waits in line, and gets "wanded" as she makes her way to the terminal to wait for her seat in coach class? Don't be silly. There are matters of security and a busy schedule to attend to the needs of her subjects (*I mean constituents*). If Members of Congress lived like us, there might be changes in that process... but they don't.

They don't even pay for most of their flights home – they are entitled to 32 per year. They don't pay for parking, nor do they drive around to look for a space. They have free parking in a special, convenient location at both Dulles and National Airports. That would change if they lived like we do. They would learn about "long-term" and "short-term" parking.

Members often fly first class – after all, they can use the upgrades they get from the frequent flyer miles they accumulate as taxpayer expense. I guess they *could* donate them to Make-a-Wish Foundation. *Right.*

There have been rule changes to disallow Members from flying on private jets owned by lobbyists, but Members always have loopholes. They fly plenty of private corporate or military jets still. You don't see them sitting in cramped seats in coach class; but you would if they lived like the rest of us.

Members should be barred from using limousines too. They can use rental cars, like we do, and take the bus to the rental lot 5 miles away. And stand in line. Like we do. If they do want a limo for a special occasion, like an anniversary dinner, they can hire one and pay for it out of their own pocket – like we do.

Vacation
In 2007, Members of the House spent 190 days in session and Senators spent 164. The rest of the time, they could conceivably spend on vacation. Of course they don't – they take care of constituent business and raise money for re-election and such. But they could just go on vacation. They often do, but they call it "official business." They travel the globe on "official business" or fact-finding missions. They can bring their spouses and kids and friends and make it an un-official party. If they lived like the rest of us, they'd get two weeks off a year and spend the rest of time in their congressional or local offices dealing with the mess they have created of our country. If they wanted a travel holiday, they'd pay for it – as would their family and friends.

And there's more

Special Perks
Do you belong to a gym? Private pool and spa? The Members do – for $100 a year. If they lived like us, there would be no exclusive subsidized recreation center; they would have to just join a gym like the rest of us - public showers and all.

Remember Senator Reid sitting ringside at the boxing championship in Las Vegas? I'm sure he's not alone in being awarded special tickets and seating for such events. If Members lived like us, they'd buy their tickets at the going rate, know what a "scalper" is, and sit in the best seats they could afford (which would be a lot less desirable on $50 thousand a year).

Those discounts in Capitol Hill tax-free shops and restaurants would have to change too – to the same rates we all pay. If they want a discount, they can fight the lines at the next Macy's sale. No more cheap meals in the private dining room either – there are plenty of restaurants in D.C. No more $10 haircuts at the congressional barbershop (though I doubt most would use John Edwards' stylist). You pay for flowers – Members should too. No more free flowers from the National Botanical Gardens.

Office Expenses

House Members are entitled to a personnel allowance from which they may hire up to 18 full-time staff members, an expense allowance consisting of a base amount plus adjustments for prevailing rents in the district and travel distance between Washington and the district, and a mail allowance based on the number of non-business addresses in the district. In 2005 amounts tended to range between $1.2 and $1.4 million per member. No telling how many friends and family are part of that package. Members have access to free congressionally owned and operated video and film studios to record messages for constituents. *Don't we all?* I don't begrudge Members having an allowance for legitimate expenses, but they should have to keep track of them just like they expect us to! They don't.

Retirement

Contrary to popular belief, Members of Congress pay into Social Security (at least they did starting in 1982). Then it gets better – of course.

They have the option of participating in one of two pension plans, depending upon when they were elected. They have a more generous formula than that offered to most other government workers. They, of course, have a more generous plan that the rest of us. They pay about 1/5 of the typical lifetime benefit; taxpayers foot the bill for the rest.

With service of 20-25 years, a Member of Congress could retire with up to 80 percent of his or her final salary. That could be as young as age 45-50. With Cost of Living Adjustments, total payments over a lifetime are often $1-2 million (some reaching $5 million). Their cushy retirement is many times more than an average citizen and much more than most high-paid executives.

What they should get is simple: social security on the same formula as all citizens and with the same retirement age. Period. If they want more, they can save and invest like the rest of us. And work to age 65 or 67 or whatever they keep raising the retirement age to.

Taxes
Why worry about an obscene tax code of 70,000 pages? The IRS maintains two "customer service centers" to assist lawmakers and Capitol Hill employees in filling out their tax forms. Taxpayers' cost for this perk is $100,000. Worse, it provides no incentive for the Members to scrap the current abominable system because they don't deal with it. One survey indicated that 60 percent of the Members of the House Ways and Means and Senate Finance Committees, who are responsible for our tax laws, didn't even prepare their own tax returns. They should be required to do so – without any outside assistance.

Special Obligations
Members of Congress should have a justifiably higher standard of behavior due to the unique position of trust and power they occupy. They should be under closer scrutiny than the rest of us since the power to abuse is so pervasive. They are not.

Direct Benefits
Many members of Congress receive farm subsidies. Senator R. Jon Tester (D-MT) and his wife own T-bone Farms, Inc., in Montana. Between 1995 and 2005, the farm received $232,311 in subsidies for oats, wheat, barley, and dry peas and assistance for miscellaneous disasters. *And you wonder why subsidies continue?*

Members should be ineligible for any public benefits, grants, or subsidies while in office. Members should be barred from voting or serving on any committee dealing with matters in which they or their families have a personal interest or possible benefit.

Investments
No one knows how much Members have benefited from "well-timed" investments armed with information from hearings, investigations and other "official business." The same is true with their connections to lobbyists and personal "friends." *Think: Hillary and commodities trades.* Members of Congress should be required to report to the public any

sales or purchases of property or investments of any type on the day of the transaction, and disclose any actual or pending legislation with a potential impact. They should not benefit from special information by virtue of their elected positions – we don't.

Military Service
If it were up to me, I would require military service as a qualification to serve in the Congress. Those with the power to make war should have served themselves. Absent a constitutional amendment, that likely wouldn't fly. But Members should at least be required to prominently and publicly disclose military service records, if any. Then we'll at least know who among them can say, "Yes, I served."

Education
Members of Congress continue to meddle in education. Then they send their own kids to private schools. An estimated 37-47% do so according to a Heritage Foundation study, and the rest presumably attend public schools (but only the best of schools, rest assured). They should be required to send their kids to the lowest performing school in the district in which they live. Then you might see some changes – like getting the federal government out of education and returning to local control by parents, teachers, and school boards.

Profit From Office
The real reason why Members spend so much of others' money to get elected is that life after office is so lucrative.

Former President Bill Clinton came to office like many – poor. He left deeply in debt, thanks to his many legal foibles. He has collected nearly $40 million in speaking fees over the past six years, according to interviews and financial disclosure statements filed by his wife, Sen. Hillary Rodham Clinton (D-N.Y) according to the Washington Post. He is but one example. Most in Congress do much better while in office, but they generally server longer and have fewer legal squabbles. They do very well. But when they do finally leave, they do much, much better.

Members of Congress should be barred from giving speeches or selling books for profit, directly or through their "libraries," foundations or trusts for five years after leaving office. The same limit should apply to sitting on boards of public corporations, employment as lobbyists or as public employees. Members are supposed to have served the public trust - not to have positioned themselves for personal gain or benefit.

Term Limits

The ultimate answer to having Members of Congress live like the rest of us is to *be* like the rest of us. We have to return to the principle that politics is about service, not employment. It should be for a limited tenure, followed by a politician's return to civilian life to live by laws he or she created. As it is now, life as a Member of Congress is far too sweet to ever want to leave. If the proposals made in this article were enacted, however, it might not be! And living like the rest of us would greatly diminish the enticing reasons to stay.

§

CHANGE
Oh Really? *(SEP 2008)*

"There is nothing wrong with change, if it is in the right direction"
~ Winston Churchill

Barack Obama has built his entire campaign for the presidency on a hollow promise of "change" and an equally ethereal appeal to "hope." Any intelligent person listening to his statements and reading his web site policy proclamations can see that there is no change in this candidate – only more of the same tired ideas advanced (and too often implemented) by Liberals over the past 75 years. His partner in "change?" - a 36-year "resident" of the Washington beltway establishment. Senator Biden seems a decent guy – but he has been part of the problem; one of the 535 Members of Congress who are responsible for the decline of this country; one of those deemed worthy by 9-14% of the citizens. He does not represent "change" – and neither does Obama.

Obama is a champion of "change" only if one considers as change:
• Increasing the already over-empowered role of the federal government.
• Increasing taxes and spending to fund huge programs for which the government is neither responsible nor effective.
• Expanding the interference of government in the lives of citizens, and diminishing personal responsibility.
• Diminishing the nation's military capacity.
• Sacrificing United States sovereignty to those who would violate our borders and to interference by international bodies such as the United Nations.
• Making U.S. foreign policy subservient to the wishes of fair-weather allies such as France and Germany.
• Catering to every special interest group imaginable in pandering for approval.
... and this is just the beginning.

Energy

Obama wants to provide "short term" relief from gas prices by robbing the strategic petroleum reserves designed for emergency needs – *such as war.* He wants to dictate that electric cars be utilized by Americans, regardless of the marketplace choices. He wants to rely on wind and solar, despite the fact that neither of these sources is economically viable without huge government subsidies. He wants to implement a "cap and trade" program which will be devastating to the economy and with huge profit windfalls for insiders such as Al Gore. He wants to socialize energy costs, giving to the chosen and government defined needy while taking from someone else.

Real Change: Open up all of America's natural resources for exploration and development by private enterprise. Stop restrictions and eliminate red-tape on business that limit, prolong and increase the expense of developing our resources. In the short term, drill for oil and use clean coal - those resources are there... at home. In the mid-term, build nuclear power plants. In the long term, work to develop hydrogen fuel cells. There, was that so hard?

Education

Obama's proposal? As usual, more federal government interference into what is a local and state issue, vastly increased spending, and interference with parental choice by getting government involved from cradle to commencement. He wants government paid support beginning at birth; government paid pre-school, government paid daycare; and free college for all. His approach favors social engineering rather than academic achievement.

Real Change: Get the federal government out of the education business altogether and allow states, communities and local school districts to function, innovate and flourish without federal bureaucracy. Abolish the Department of Education and all federal funding for education. It's not their job. Stop enrolling illegal residents in American schools. Stop sending unqualified and unmotivated kids to college.

Economy

Obama's idea of change? More federal money: grants, subsidies, incentives, rebates, benefits, and other social and business tinkering. Government has never created a job, seldom invented or discovered anything (with the exception of military and space programs), and rarely created wealth or well-being for anyone - except politicians. The success of this country is based on capitalism – and Obama's programs are designed to interfere with, not enhance, its functioning.

Real Change: Cut government spending, cut government bureaucracy, cut government meddling, and let capitalism work to create jobs and wealth for Americans. Implement trade policies that are favorable to the U.S., not damaging to it. Stop burdening businesses with personal responsibilities for health care, unemployment, family needs, and other socialist agenda items. *We can take care of ourselves.*

Culture

Obama wants to expand "hate crimes," (crime is crime), end racial profiling, and continue the trend toward making everyone a victim. Obama supports marriage between homosexuals, despite overwhelming nationwide rejection of the concept. He wants equal pay based on gender and race, not performance. He wants to fund faith-based organizations with public money, despite our nation's constitutional "separation of church and state." Presumably, this would include Muslim organizations and hate-mongering churches such as that run by Jeremiah Wright.

Real Change: Stop social engineering by the government while protecting the constitutional right to life, liberty, and the pursuit of happiness for all citizens. Only the pursuit is guaranteed – not the result.

Health care

Obama wants to do for health care what government has done for education – screw it up. The United States has the best health care system and the best providers in the world. That standing is increasingly under pressure due to government interference, health insurance company meddling, and trial attorneys, all of which add to the cost of providing care. Government driven bureaucrats like Obama operate under the delusion that "free" anything doesn't require someone else paying for it.

Real Change: Return to a health care system run by medical professionals, not government and insurance company bureaucrats. Limit ridiculous legal awards. Fund "safety net" basic medical costs through a state – not federal – add-on to sales tax so the burden is equally and easily shared by all, including the recipients of care. Stop paying for the health care of illegal residents and their families.

Immigration

If 2 million Chinese or Russians showed up on our borders, we would consider it an attack on America. Obama thinks that 20 million illegal entrants, largely from Mexico and Central America, coming hundreds at a time should be tolerated. He thinks they, and their families, should be accommodated and invited to become citizens. Under his vision of "change" and a supportive Democratic Congress, they will. He wants to provide more economic development to Mexico, without reciprocation – a carrot, but not stick. He supports the incorrect interpretation of the Constitution allowing citizenship to children of Illegals, and wants to ensure rewarding them by allowing other family members to join them.

Real Change: Deport those who have entered the country illegally, strengthen the means of identifying and apprehending Illegals. Stop rewarding illegal entry with education, health care, citizenship, and family unification. Make foreign countries responsible for their citizens and the costs of both illegal entry and removal. Reform legal immigration to favor those coming here with assets, sponsors, education, English speaking skills, and a dedication to American principles, culture and values. Prohibit immigration or entry from terrorist supporting nations.

Taxes and spending

Obama's proposals – and this is just the beginning – will cost over $1 trillion. The budget will likely not be balanced, and to the extent it is, it will come from vastly increased taxes and fees, a decimation of the military, and other essential needs to support feel-good social programs. As Democrats have shown in their control of Congress over the past two years, earmarks and other wasteful spending will increase, not decrease. He will continue the class warfare of the past, blaming "the wealthy" for their greed and selfishness. (Note: those with incomes in the top 5% pay 60% of personal income taxes; the bottom 50% pay 2.9%.) He will chastise "big oil," "big drug companies," and successful businesses for being profitable (increasing the wealth of shareholders), creating jobs (increasing the wealth of individuals), and creating new inventions and discoveries (increasing the wealth and well-being of society and the world).

Real Change: Drastically cut the size of the federal government by restoring roles reserved to the states. Prohibit earmarks and other spending attachments and allow only items relevant to a bill to be associated with it. Install term limits to ensure that personal fiefdoms are not created, feeding the self-interest of politicians and catering to special interest groups. Dismantle the IRS and the income tax system and implement a sales tax only system in which all citizens participate simply, fairly and directly. The wealthy will pay more because they spend more. Even Jesse Jackson's "non-profit" organizations will contribute. Stop the free lunch mentality and return to a concept of personal responsibility – not government handouts.

Politics
Barack Obama has raised $390 million for his presidential campaign. This money did not come from housewives in Iowa. He has taken money from corporations, unions, lobbyists (not directly, of course), George Soros, "bundlers" and other sources. He has taken huge amounts of money over the Internet from "who knows where?" He believes in campaign finance reform. *Right.* He supports improving ethics – who doesn't (at least in theory). He will foster the typical bureaucracy of reform, while turning a blind eye to the reality.

Real Change: Prohibit contributions to political candidates from any source except verified (by valid ID reference) U.S. citizens. Prohibit contributions within 30 days of an election. Require public posting within 24 hours (via the internet) of all contributions from any single or related source over $1,000 and within 5 days for all other amounts.

Military

Obama wants to end the war in Iraq – right idea, wrong rationale. He will likely want to send troops to Darfur and Georgia. Liberals don't end wars; they simply change the venue. He wants to stop new weapons systems development and pursue nuclear disarmament. I'm sure we can trust Russia, Iran, China and Korea to all comply in total honesty. He wants young people to volunteer for soup kitchens as if that were the equivalent of service in the armed forces. Then again, why would he expect something he himself has not done? He will pay for his vast increase in social programs the same way Bill Clinton did – by massive reductions in our country's military capacity and readiness. *Great change.*

Real Change: Restore America as a nation to be feared and respected for fair and legitimate protection of its citizens and national interests. Insist that allies provide fully for their own defense and support U.S. intervention when justified. Return to a universal military service obligation, including politicians and their children. War drums beat less loudly when one has a personal stake.

Foreign policy

Obama wants to increase the role of the United Nations, cater to the self-interests of France and other "allies," and save Africa from itself. He thinks we have a moral duty to rescue the Third World from AIDS, poverty and hunger with the dollars of Americans, taken without their consent. He thinks dialogue is the answer to gaining respect with nations rooted in fanaticism, hatred and evil. One again wonders where all those Internet campaign contributions came from? No doubt they were all U.S. citizens. Is his foreign policy really foreign payback?

Real Change: Parity – it's that simple. We give as good as we get. We retain our sovereign rights and duties and expect other nations to do the same. We are not bound by any international organization whose authority exceeds that of our U.S. Constitution. We support the humanitarian efforts of private citizens, but do not take from them for any purpose not consti-tutionally defined (including all foreign aid). We work with other nations to defend themselves, eradicate disease, feed their people and prosper economically – we do not do that *for* them.

There is no change - except for the worse

Barack Obama is not about change. He is the embodiment – the zenith – of liberal thinking that has not changed in 80 years. That mindset operates in a world filled with guilt over the success of this country and an unjustified craving for approval by the rest of world, despite the rest of the world's general inferiority in achievement. It honors form over substance, appearance over reality, and feelings over reason. This type of "change" requires as many victims as possible to justify invading the lives of the self-supporting to rob them of the fruits of their hard work and achievement. The objective is not individual freedom to seek happiness, but government engineering to produce equal outcomes.

The Barack Obamas of the world want to force you to drive a sub-compact electric car while they are transported in limos and private jets. They voice false concern over your basic housing needs, while they occupy mansions acquired through the gifts or financial assistance of others. They feel guilty over attending posh colleges, so they want you to pay for others to do the same. They seek office not to serve, but to control.

Obama and other Liberals are not about change. They have never changed; their goals have never changed; their methods are the same as always. The only change they stand for is in making your life change to their perception of what it should be. We don't need that kind of change. If we get it, there is no "hope" for America as we know it.

§

HOW REPUBLICANS WIN
... Or keep losing *(MAY 2009)*

"Governments are republican only in proportion as they employ the will of the people and execute it"
> *~ Thomas Jefferson*

L et's make one thing clear: I'm not a fan of either party at this point. The problems we face as a country and within our states are not simply the problems of the Democrats or the Republicans – they are the problems of both parties; of government as a whole; of a self-serving political elite.

I remain a registered Republican only because I view them, as a whole, as the lesser of the two evils - with at least some potential for redemption (though I don't have high hopes). The change of party by Arlen Specter to the Democrats was not significant in itself. The shame was that Republicans continued to support him for as long as they did! He should have been thrown out of the Party long ago – along with Olympia Snowe and a few others who hardly qualify for the Republican label. I'd rather be a minority Party with principles than a majority one without.

There are many pundits who claim the Republicans can survive only by moving to the left; by becoming more "moderate." I am not among them. *That* suggestion is, in fact, the reason they are losing. They are no longer a choice, but an echo, despite Goldwater's advice to the contrary in 1964. They can never win by being "Democrat-lite;" they need bold ideas and programs. They need to be right. Here's how:

1. Abolish the IRS and the income tax
This country does not need another tax "reform" act. It does not need to add to the 70,000 page, 6-million word travesty that has become our tax code. Government will give up huge power and control and citizens will regain their freedom when the IRS and the current tax system are abolished. Repeal the 16th Amendment and institute a consumption tax only system.

The F.A.I.R. Tax program is one place to start. Repeat the process at the state level of every state. This is the one most important thing Republicans can do to assert a commitment to freedom, liberty, and a respect for our constitutional principles.

2. Limit government

Government at all levels has become obscenely enmeshed in every aspect of our lives; it long ago exceeded the legitimate bounds of its usefulness. It is time for major restructuring of government, not token remodeling, but demolition with a wrecking ball. Half the cabinet functions in the executive branch need to be abolished and government returned to the limited and specified purposes stated in the Constitution. Functions not the role of the federal government such as education and health care should be transferred to the states.

The role of government in the economy should be restricted to facilitating and preserving operation of the system of capitalism, not socialist tinkering with the government injecting itself into businesses. Regulations need to be slashed and barriers to entry or growth removed to allow businesses to do what they do: create jobs, provide needed products and services, and create wealth. Government needs to get out of their way! When companies become too successful, whether through overly successful competition or unfair practices, they need to be broken up into competitive units so that capitalism can be re-established. No company should be allowed to become "too big to fail."

The role of the federal government will be reduced when elected federal representatives lose their "Beltway" mentality and return to the states that they represent. By repealing the 17th Amendment, U.S. Senators would once again return their focus to state service, not national power. They should be based in their home state capitals, as well, not ensconced in the insulated life of privilege and Georgetown parties.

When the size of government is cut, so will the numbers and influence of lobbyists and special interests. Republicans can go a step further by banning elected officials from serving as lobbyists for 5 years after they leave office. They can also name names of wives and other ties to elected officials serving as lobbyists or other influence peddlers making their unseemly activities open to public scrutiny. It shouldn't be the sole job of talk radio and TV hosts to expose questionable ties and activities to the light of day!

3. Cap spending and limit deficits
Money is the life-blood of government. Cut off the money supply and you cut the ability of government to grow beyond justifiable limits. The budgets of federal, state and local government need to be capped. Federal spending should be capped at, say, 15% of GDP and states at perhaps 10-15% of GSP (Gross State Product), with an allocation to local governments by formula. Federal deficits should not be allowed except during periods of *declared* national emergency or war.

4. Implement term limits
Political service is not a job. It should be limited, and those serving regularly returned to civilian life to live by the system they have helped create. That system is broken when it comes to limiting time in office. The re-election rate to Congress has been regularly above 90% for decades, despite 14% approval ratings and ruination of the country by these tired, egotistical fools. They have stacked the deck, and it is time for a new deck: *term limits*. Two terms in the Senate, four terms in the House – that's it. Since service is limited, elected officials no longer deserve lavish pensions. They can live on their personal retirement programs and social security, like the rest of us. Since no one serves for 30-40 years, we can stop elevating doddering fools to "seniority" and instead use valid qualifications and new ideas as the basis for chairing committees. There should be *no* grandfathering. Those having served past the enacted term limits should be forced to resign at the end of their terms. Yes, Republicans, this means limiting your own terms too!

5. Revise and enforce immigration policy
Immigration, legal and illegal, is a major problem for the country. It will not be fixed simply or quickly. We can start by putting illegal residents on notice that they will no longer be eligible for public education, health care,

or other benefits. They will not be criminalized or hunted down; they will simply not be rewarded. If they are found to be here illegally, they will be limited or excluded from future consideration for legal entry; they must know there is a price to pay. We will enforce the Constitution so that babies born here to illegal residents are no longer automatic citizens; they are citizens – and the responsibility – of their native country. We will negotiate treaties with other countries to enforce these rules.

Legal immigration will return to policies favoring those who embrace the traditional language and culture of America; who have basic economic capacity and sponsors; and who possess reasonable education or trade skills. We will admit numbers that can be reasonably adsorbed into the fabric of America and those who want to assimilate it. We will not admit those from terrorist or terrorist harboring states, nor consider them for temporary or student visas. Period.

6. Protect culture
Support those measures, programs and way of life that reflect our native culture as an English-speaking nation of western European traditions and legal systems, based on Christian philosophy and values. Foster respect for other cultures without sacrificing and making subservient our own. Preserve the right of personal choice in private behaviors and lifestyles, while rejecting public endorsement of those behaviors and practices outside our traditional mainstream.

7. Restrict internationalism
Establish the protection and best interests of this nation as the only basis on which to conduct international relations and policy. There is no constitutional or moral duty to assist other nations for any other purposes. If it is in the best interests of this nation to act then we should, if it is not, we should not. If we enter into alliances, they should be two-way and mutually beneficial. Our partners need to support us and pay their way to peace, not ride for free in our tanks, ships and planes or on the backs of U.S. soldiers.

8. Scrap foreign aid

It is not the duty of U.S. taxpayers to fund foreign countries or governments. Our government can serve as a conduit for the flow of funds volunteered by Americans for humanitarian or other justifiable purposes. It should never be simply taken from them for unjustified goals, no matter how well intended. Americans are kind and giving people, but that role should never be assumed for them or without their consent.

9. Return sanity to law

Reform the legal system to reduce the number of laws, and rid our books of outmoded, unfair or onerous laws. Stop criminalizing society with incarceration for minor offenses and personal choices, while allowing whole cities to fall prey to control of gangs and true criminals. Put law enforcement back into the hands of local jurisdictions.

10. Send the right messenger

None of the above will matter if the messenger isn't up to the challenge of delivering the message. Stop focusing on the party faithful and start looking for the dynamic, youthful and eloquent spokesman who can articulate the message of the future, not hollow reverberations of past failures.

Conclusion

These are the messages that will win Americans. These are real messages, not lofty generalities of the type still being espoused by the big government people in power. Their message is designed to appeal to those who don't pay for the cost of government, and who often benefit directly from it or are employed by it. The ones who DO pay for it don't have the votes, though they still have the power. But they are running out of time, and the Republican approach of the past decade is letting them down.

Republicans need to play hardball. They are bullied and beaten and try to take the "moral high ground." That won't work – this is war! The mainstream media is not their friend. The union dominated education/public employee bureaucracy is not their friend. The celebrities of pop culture are not their friends. The special interests who love the benefits of big government are not their friends. Recognize these facts, accept them, and deal with them realistically.

Do *not* send Sarah Palin to a "friendly" interview with Katie Couric. Tell Katie to go pound salt. When the media pokes fun at Gov. Palin for commenting that she can see Russia from Alaska, point out – repeatedly – that yes, Alaska is one of the 50 - not 57 - states Obama claims to have visited. In fact, repeat the stupid gaffes made by this president over and over until he appears as dunce-like as the Liberal edia made George Bush appear to be. Fight fire with fire, not marshmallows.

Do *not* simply let pass the shady associations of Barack Obama or the questions of suitability of his appointments. We know too well that the opposition would not be so kind. They are *still* trying to find something to hang on Dick Cheney. So much for "moving on."

When the Leftists talk of the fairness doctrine in radio or the need for affirmative action to ensure equality of opposing messages, remind them that 90% of educators as well as the Washington Press Corps are self-described Liberals. Remind them too of the overwhelming left bias of major newspapers and network television. Don't be afraid to talk honestly, openly and fairly about issues of race, gender and other "sensitive" issues. *People aren't stupid.*

When Obama talks about supporting public education, remind the public that he sends his kids to an elite private school. When the Democrat Congress talks about health care for the masses, remind the masses of the special health system serving Congress. Point out that thousands of veterans fail to receive medical care, while non-veteran Congressmen have access to Walter Reed and the Bethesda Naval Hospital.

Expose the hypocrisy of Leftists including Hollywood elite, George Soros and wealthy Members of Congress. Talk about how Harry Reid rose from obscurity in Searchlight to become a wealthy land baron worth perhaps $60 million – on a politician's salary. Talk about the $billions shelled out by

Dianne Feinstein to her husband's company while she approved contracts on the defense subcommittee she chaired for years. Talk about the wealth and lifestyles of Pelosi, Boxer, Kerry and Kennedy – the great champions of the "average" American.

Challenge the surveys that tell us that 50% of Americans want to pay more taxes, but fail to point that the same number pay little or no tax at all! Challenge all the conventional wisdom as well as the obviously biased assertions of the Left. But most of all, challenge yourselves. If you ever again fall into the trap of listening to and even nominating another John McCain, your party is toast. Quit the club of elite political self-interest and re-join the American people or someone else will take over for you - another party, or the people themselves.

§

WHAT CONSERVATISM *ISN'T* (NOV 2003)

"Any man who is under 30, and is not a liberal, has not heart; and any man who is over 30, and is not a conservative, has no brains."
~ *Winston Churchill*

The major print media, television, and other left-leaning groups regularly characterize Conservatives as out of the mainstream on contemporary issues. They are variously described as mean-spirited, racist, homophobic, anti-women, pro-business, anti-environment, and just plain bad. Conservatives are identified as favoring the wealthy, stepping on the poor, and overlooking the elderly.

The ongoing campaign is clearly intended to stifle debate on any of the real issues, and limit the stage to those ideas presented by Liberal Leftists. The effort is working for many Americans since the Liberal Ideologues have garnered control of many major influences on popular thought and culture, despite their rejection of reason, justice, and common sense. The education establishment has been largely taken over by Liberals, as has the elite television and print media; there is nary a Conservative to be found in the entertainment industry, and Conservatives bear the brunt of jokes and derision.

The best way to respond to mischaracterization of what conservatism is, is to accurately identify what it isn't, accusations of major media, Liberals, and left wing groups notwithstanding.

Conservatism isn't "intolerant."
To maintain a steadfast allegiance to a philosophy believed correct is not intolerance. To the extent other points of view are not in conflict with that philosophy, they are respected even though different. But to surrender one's beliefs to an opposing and perhaps conflicting point of view is not tolerant; it simply shows a lack of conviction. To the degree such surrender affects fundamental beliefs, it can be fatal. A popular expression says it all: *"A person who stands for nothing, will fall for anything."*

Conservatism isn't "mean-spirited."
The term "compassionate Conservative" was coined to counter the idea that somehow conservatism is mean and uncaring. Liberals would call this an oxymoron; I would call it a redundancy. Caring and compassion are personal values, not fixed to a particular ideology. Conservatives simply believe that the most genuine form of caring for those less fortunate is to help them to help themselves, not to be dependent on government or handouts. Which approach is truly the less compassionate: one that fuels self-esteem, accomplishment, and self-determination or one that chains generation after generation to the public dole (confiscated from the hard working folks who pay the bills)?

Conservatism isn't "rich, white and male"
Conservatism doesn't derive from economic status, race, or sex; it is a philosophy based on reason, justice, and common sense. It seeks an environment in which all are free to participate, compete, and achieve based on their God-given talents, their own labors, and their own risks and choices. The outcomes are not preordained; they are earned. If many Conservatives turn out to be successful, white and male, it is simply because they have chosen a path open to all, but taken only by the few.

Conservatism isn't racist
Conservatives reject the notion that anyone is limited by race; they insist that each of us is capable of pursuing and realizing our dreams, constrained only by our physical limits. For that reason, racial preferences, quotas, "affirmative action," and other programs which assume an inability to achieve based on race are considered both wrong and offensive. They are a slap in the face to those seeking to achieve and they diminish the accomplishment of those who have.

Conservatism isn't "anti-woman"
Conservatives respect women and womanhood as a unique gift to humanity. Whether dedicated to motherhood and family life, pursuing a career in any number of fields, or both, the potential for achievement by women is no different than by men. Conservatives do not, however, deny

the common sense recognition that men and women have inherent differences that often favor certain paths in life. That general observation in no way limits *any* individual to pursue a course less conventional. Every woman is free to choose, and free to succeed.

Conservatism isn't homophobic

Like most personal behaviors, conservatism differentiates between public and private conditions. There is tolerance for private matters of a behavioral nature, no matter what one's view as to the rightness or wrongness of it. This is the point radical homosexuals can't seem to get: keep it to yourself and no one cares; flaunt it as a public issue and it becomes publicly debatable based on community standards and norms. The belief that homosexuality is abnormal, unnatural, and morally offensive to many people is factual; the acceptance or tolerance of it as private behavior is simply a reasoned and just choice. It is not hateful, irrational, fearful, or phobic to view homosexuality in this perspective. It is simply another point of view to which people are entitled.

Conservatism isn't "anti-immigrant"

There are basically three types of immigrants: (1) those who come here legally, seeking to be Americans, and to assimilate American language, culture and way of life; to pledge their allegiance to this great nation; and to contribute to its growth and take of its opportunities through their efforts; (2) those who come here legally, but simply seek to export their prior language and culture; to take of America's fruits; and (3) those who come here illegally for mere economic opportunity, either from their own labor; from the generosity of the welfare state; or worse, to participate in crime or terrorist activities. Conservatism celebrates the first group; it reluctantly tolerates the second; and it rejects outright the third. Conservatism isn't anti-immigrant; it is pro-America.

Conservatism isn't "anti-education"

Conservatives are generally strong supporters of education, including public education. But when public education becomes indoctrination it is rejected rightly as intrusive and antithetical to the true ends of education.

When education becomes the ward of the federal government instead of the child of the local community, it suffers, and Conservatives reject that too. When endless streams of money produce neither improvements nor even basic competence, Conservatives are not afraid to question and demand change. *By the way, where do all those Liberals in Washington D.C. send their kids to school?* Yes, exclusive private schools almost without exception – so much for intellectual honesty.

Conservatism isn't "anti-environment"
Many Conservatives are hunters and fishermen, and are among the most committed and effective environmentalists. Conservatives support policies that protect scarce natural resources, and have a reverence for nature in general. Why is it in fact that so many Conservatives live in the country, while so many Liberals live in cities? Who's kidding whom? Conservatives believe that mankind is part of the environment, however, and has a legitimate claim to natural resources for its own benefit. They believe in protecting all life forms, but legitimately question the "species of the day" that surfaces every time a building permit is about to be pulled… especially when it is an insect (about 6 million species as I recall), or a weed.

Conservatism isn't "anti-privacy"
Quite the contrary, Conservatives are greatly troubled by invasions of privacy, in both the public and private sectors. As with other philo-sophical views, they prefer to deal in substance and reason, rather than innuendo and emotion. The most deeply held beliefs regarding privacy and personal freedoms are those defined by our Founders – which are regularly trampled by liberal judges to redefine the rights of one at the expense of another.

Conservatism isn't "anti-government"
Conservatism supports the necessity of government sufficient to accomplish those essential reasons for its existence. In the case of the federal government, those reasons are quite specific and limited by the Constitution - and they have been grossly exceeded. In the case of state and

local governments, the Conservative's complaint is that they have failed to preserve their constitutionally reserved domains, while expanding into other areas beyond their legitimate authority. It is the imbalance in government which offends the sensibilities of Conservatives. They are not anti-government; they just want government restored to its limited and defined role.

Now, this exercise won't prevent the Liberals from asserting falsehoods about conservatism. Accuracy and honesty is not part of their equation. It is more compatible with the Liberal agenda to define conservatism for what it needs it to *be* to justify their own agenda, rather than to recognize it for what it really *is*.

§

FAILED SYSTEMS
Education

"We are faced with the paradoxical fact that education has become one of the chief obstacles to intelligence and freedom of thought."
~ Bertrand Russell

EDUCATED IDIOTS (NOV 2005)

Something has happened to education over the past 50 years, and it can hardly be called progress. We have more people with college degrees than ever, yet many of them are functionally high school dropouts. An 8th grade education in the 1930s produced an arguably greater breadth of knowledge and superior capacity for basic academics, including math, science, history and communication in English.

At the same time, we are told that we must accept the labor of illegal immigrants because American workers won't fill the needed jobs. In fact, many jobs that Americans won't fill are quite well paid, but don't require an advanced education. I recently checked into having some wallpaper hung in my office – 2 rooms and a bathroom. Only two individuals in the whole of northwest Nevada, it seems, could perform this modest job. The cost quoted was over $1,800 – not including the paper! Now this was about a day and a half job so the wages earned were not exactly minimum wage. Has it occurred to some marginally qualified college bound kid (and his or her parents) that both the demand and the rewards for hanging wallpaper are quite high? This is not to denigrate fields such as the social sciences and fine arts; we need those too. But we direct too many into subjects of academic curiosity, while ignoring fields that meet daily needs and create wealth: farming, building, engineering, mathematics, science... and paper hanging.

We have become a nation of educated idiots, while our ability to fill jobs with skilled workers has declined well below our needs. The two problems are closely entwined. Let's look at the players.

High School students used to come to school neatly dressed, bright eyed, and prepared – well, perhaps not always, but on most days. They had few distractions, such as cell phones. Strange hair-dos or pants falling off would be a guaranteed ticket back home. The school day ran from 8 a.m. to 3:30 p.m. and generally included 5-6 "solid" subjects and PE. Curricula were comprised of historically recognized – and proven sequences of instruction. In math, for example: Algebra I, Plane Geometry, Algebra II, Trigonometry, Solid Geometry and Calculus. English was the sole language of instruction, and students were expected to master both the written and spoken form.

Today's students arrive looking like slobs, bleary-eyed from watching music videos or playing video games until midnight, and still plugged into their electronic devices even in the classroom. The school day and curriculum have been revised endlessly so that classroom time is minimal and course offerings are barely recognizable. We have dual tracks, alternating schedules, and a school day that ends about 1 pm! Subjects are more cotton candy than steak and potatoes, and performance is measured by how well one *tries*, not how well *does*. More time is spent teaching in languages other than English, or meeting "special needs," while the "general needs" of the majority are ignored. A focus on group and team effort masks the lack of accomplishment by the individual. Some coast on the efforts of others, while a few truly excel on their own. Students are passed on from one level to the next, regardless of performance, and the system is "dumbed down" lest we damage the self-image of non-performing students by intimating that they are lazy, unaccomplished, or both. Students are taught that failure *is* an option.

Teachers used to dress professionally and act the same. They were committed to teaching as a profession, not merely a job protected by labor unions and tenure. Their focus was on academic achievement at the highest level – not simply that which was good enough. Among the best, they helped groom, motivate, and develop brilliance. For those less capable, they imparted a sense of confidence and basic skills to function as good and productive citizens. Teachers today often take more pride in being a "friend," rather than an example. They nurture free expression, at the expense of knowledge. Teachers seldom make demands for more control, higher standards, or improved performance - only more money and less work. To be sure, there are still many dedicated and talented teachers but they appear to be an increasing minority.

Education functioned well when it involved students, parents and teachers, with an occasional administrator to deal with planning and discipline. Teachers had absolute authority and responsibility in the classroom, and principals had the same school-wide. Private schools still tend to run on that paradigm – and function better in general. Declines in public education performance have been aggravated further by the increased involvement of government - especially federal bureaucrats. To those 3,000 miles away from reality, performance is a statistical summary of test scores, however manipulated, to achieve the desired result. Get government out of education, and watch it improve.

If the problems in K-12 education are extensive, they reach a zenith in higher education. Egos and power prevail, with plenty of support from politicians wanting to be the "education candidate." No one seems to notice the ever expanding landscape of expensive college buildings; the swollen faculties pregnant with those "teaching" pure folly; or the hordes of students enrolled in remedial classes, with few completing a college program in the traditional 4-year time frame. In fact, perhaps a third to half of the students enrolled in college would be better off getting jobs.

Colleges are full of educated idiots, while carpenters, electricians, plumbers – and paperhangers – are in scarce supply. Maybe higher education isn't so high up on the value scale in society after all – at least not for everyone. Perhaps for those seeking it, the bar needs to be raised and the effort directed into areas of greatest need – science, engineering, language, and mathematics. Perhaps we ought to revise our thoughts about education as a life skill, and not simply an endless pursuit of mediocre and esoteric academic babble. The fact is, we need more reasonably educated workers – and fewer highly educated idiots.

Here's a simple plan to reduce costs and improve quality for higher education in our state institutions. Those in the top 25% of high school by grades or test scores are allowed to enter 4-year colleges and universities. Those in the next 25% are allowed to enter 2-year community college programs. Those in the next 25% are allowed to enter vocational programs. Those in the lower 25% are encouraged to get a job. No one, of course, would be discouraged from seeking admission as they matured, demonstrated commitment, motivation, and excellence in subsequent years. All students would be encouraged to perform military service somewhere along the way, and rewarded for doing so in education scholarships on a year for year basis. *Of course, this may smack just a bit too much of common sense.*

§

FAILED SYSTEMS
Law

"Where you find the laws most numerous, there you will find also the greatest injustice."
   ~ Arcesilaus

A NATION OF (TOO MANY) LAWS (JUN 2006)

In the "Golden Rule" (do unto others as you would have them do unto you), we have a simple maxim for virtually all personal behavior - in one sentence. In the Ten Commandments, we have a basic guide for the morality of our culture - in essentially a paragraph. The Declaration of Independence provided the foundation for individual freedom and the relationship of government to the governed – *in one page*. Our United States Constitution is the model of republican democracy and the supreme law of the land – in perhaps ten pages, including the Bill of Rights. These are great documents, providing the basic guides for decency, relationships with others, and the operation of society. We have lost something in the translation of these powerful instruments into the laws which derive from them.

Compare the foregoing to the Internal Revenue Code which contains more than a million words. It has grown from 19,500 pages in 1984 to 45,662 pages in 2001 and 70,000 pages today. Since 1995, there have been 2,116 changes in federal tax law. At all levels, an average of 15,000 new laws are passed nationwide each year -*15,000!* The 2005 Nevada Legislature submitted 510 new bills – many became law under Nevada's Revised Statutes. In addition, there were "special acts," city and county ordinances, and countless agency rules and bureaucratic regulations.

Yes, we are a nation of laws – but we have become strangled by too many of them. Is freedom in jeopardy because of excess in our laws? I believe so.

One of the biggest problems is the mindset of our legislators. They think it is their job to make laws. *It is not.* Their job is to better society at the level they govern. That involves a consideration of problems and issues and the variety of *all* options available to them – not simply the creation of new laws. Consider how the problem of illegal immigration would be affected if Congress and the courts simply enforced existing laws, without the creation of new ones. In other cases, as with the tax code, the problems are compounded by too many or excessively complex laws. Solutions would be better made by reducing, simplifying, and even the wholesale abolition of laws – in this case, by enacting a simple, single sales tax system and abolishing all other tax laws. *But that would limit congressional power!*

Another problem is simply bad law; creating laws that are incomplete, vague, conflicting, or defective. Legislators then leave the task of sorting out problems to bureaucratic fixes, thereby delegating law-making to a swarm of un-elected and unaccountable agencies. The administrative rules and regulations of these agencies have the force of law and add to the nightmare that has become our legal system.

Special interests drive much legislation as payback for their financial contributions and support of candidates. When laws are narrowly drawn to benefit one person, company or sector, it is hard to justify the general benefit to society. It is not just "big" business that creates such havoc. MADD mothers, the ACLU, environmental groups, and others start with the best of intentions but their zeal invariably overcomes their reason. The result is generally an abusive crusade, not a reasonable legal restraint on unacceptable behavior.

In the area of behavior affecting ourselves, we have seen no end to laws attempting to guide, cajole, modify, or forbid. Laws affecting smoking, drinking, wearing safety gear - even eating fast food - are the tip of the iceberg. We become convinced that "the state" knows what is best for us. Much of this thinking is rooted in the state taking on responsibility for our behavior. One solution, instead of more laws, requirements and prohibitions, is for the state to simply stop taking on responsibility for personal decisions of the citizens, and the consequences thereof.

The whole range of laws based on civil rights and liberties has grown since the 1960s. While these laws purport to secure and protect the rights of one class, they invariably do so at the expense of the rights of another. What's missing is balance. Such laws are passed based on which group yells the loudest, recruits the most protestors, or is favored by the politically correct crowd. Innocuous sounding labels such as "affirmative action" belie the fact that one class is being rewarded at the expense of another. "Gay rights" is simply a euphemism for forced inculcation and acceptance of values not shared by others. By such processes, the unfair is made legally fair, the abnormal is made legally normal, and the vocal minority supplants the silent majority by legalistic stealth. Balance between rights and duties is not preserved; it is destroyed.

Whenever something exceptional happens, especially if it is something spectacular in degree or effect, laws will follow. This tendency to pass hurried laws in response to highly visible events can have costly, even dangerous, consequences. Good law derives from recognizing and dealing with the rule, not the exception; and doing so in a deliberative manner, not a knee-jerk reaction. The Patriot Act, in response to the events of 9/11 is one example. The recent Senate "immigration bill" is another. For 30 years, we failed to enforce existing laws, allowing 20 million to enter the country illegally and millions of non-citizens to go from grade school to college. Then, with little time for debate, the Senate pushed through an immigration amnesty bill of massive proportions and consequences. This is a travesty of law making.

We have become fond of putting people in jail for the smallest of infractions, or for relatively minor offenses. Our jails and prisons are bursting at the seams, lives are needlessly complicated, or even ruined; and for what purpose? The good feeling that some holier-than-thou lawmaker or bureaucrat got from punishing "evil?" At the same time, we have allowed criminal gangs to roam the streets of our cities, literally without fear of retribution, because we fail to deal with crime truly deserving of incarceration. *We go after the bunnies and let the wolves run free.*

Some Ideas for Change
The whole mind set of lawmaking has to change, beginning with the recognition that the function of the legislatures in our republic is not simply to make laws, but to make a better society.

The ability to create new legislation must be reined in. I would suggest allowing the introduction of new bills in only alternate legislative sessions. In the remaining sessions, actions would be limited to the abolition, consolidation, or simplification of existing laws. Exception could be made for emergency legislation with approval of 2/3 of the legislatures.

All new laws should have "sunset" provisions to ensure that they are truly necessary in relation to the cost of their implementation and enforcement, and after a reasonable time to allow for evaluation. Each new law passed should expire in two years (or two legislative sessions) unless re-approved by an affirmative vote of the legislature. Prior to a vote for continuation, there should be a thorough analysis of the law's economic, social, and other impacts. A second, long-term sunset provision should kick in at the 10-year anniversary of all laws, unless explicitly renewed.

Bad and excessive lawmaking is often the result of entrenched political and bureaucratic interests, with insulation from the will of the broad citizenry. The cure is breaking the lock of incumbency in elected offices and permanence among public employees. All elected officials should serve limited terms for reasonable total periods of 6-12 years. They may then either seek higher office if qualified and supported by the voters, or return to civilian life to live by the laws they have created. The thirst for the power of perpetual office is among the most corrupting influences to bad law making. So is the demand for money to hold such power. Campaign contributions need to be banned from any source except individual citizens, with full disclosure of the amounts and sources of such funds. Career bureaucrats should be rotated every so often as well, to provide a fresh look at the regulatory climate in which they operate, and avoid the mental mildew that sets in from too much time - and power - in one position.

Reading of all legislation should be mandatory, and a reasonable time allowed for such reading - say 2 weeks. The cramming through of thousands of pages of legislation and forced votes, often overnight, is a travesty to good lawmaking and to common sense.

Lastly, all laws should include citation of the constitutional authority by which they are authorized. Such a requirement has been introduced many times, but Congress keeps turning it down. What could be more reasonable? What is our political leadership afraid of? As usual, it is simply about the diminution of power that would follow from doing the right thing.

Our Republic, a nation of laws, has become a nation of far *too many* laws, and especially of bad and corrupting laws. Change is never easy, but the failure to change is far worse. Democracy as we know it is on a downslope, and a defective system of laws is assisting the decline.

"If a bureaucrat had been writing the Ten Commandments, a simple rock slab would not have had nearly enough room. Those simple rules would have read, 'Thou Shalt Not, unless you feel strongly to the contrary, or for the following stated exceptions (See Paragraphs 1-10, Subsection A).'"
   ~ Ronald Reagan

§

FAILED SYSTEMS
Capitalism

"The inherent vice of capitalism is the unequal sharing of blessings; the inherent virtue of socialism is the equal sharing of miseries."
~ *Winston Churchill*

CAPITALISM 101 (FEB 2009)

Capitalism is one the fundamental principles upon which America is based and through which it has become a great nation. Despite this, capitalism has been eroded, undermined, and even derided as an anachronism. The political elite, let by Reid, Pelosi and now, President Obama, feel that America should look to its geographic right – *Europe* - while embracing its economic left - *Socialism*.

In fact, we have been leaning leftward ever since FDR's "New Deal," propelled further by LBJ's "Great Society." We are now reaching full momentum with the "change" agenda of the Obama administration and a heavily Democrat Congress. The move to Socialism is in full swing.

A key element of socialism is nationalism. Reserving power to the states was the constitutional restraint to the advance of excess national authority upon which Socialism feeds. Consider the institutions, which have been effectively nationalized or proposed to be: media airways, education, retirement, mortgage finance, and health care. Add to the list economic sectors heavily affected by federal regulation: banking (FDIC), securities (SEC), Energy (FERC), telecommunications (FCC), and pharmaceuticals (FDA). Many sectors are also heavily dependent on federal subsidies, such as agriculture, alternative energy, and public housing.

With recent and proposed "bailouts," we are now entering an era of federal ownership of private concerns in exchange for federal funds including: banking, insurance, securities, and automobile companies. The pattern should be frightening. It is being sold as essential to our way of life; it is, in fact, its ruination.

Capitalism and freedom go hand in hand. The freedom to own property, to own one's own labor and to make personal choices are basic elements of capitalism. It is through capitalism that we create jobs and wealth, build personal and national independence, and secure the freedom to rise or fall without regard to birth class. As Winston Churchill said: *"The inherent vice of capitalism is the uneven division of blessings, while the inherent virtue of socialism is the equal division of misery."* The further difference, however, is that the former is a matter of personal choice, while the latter is imposed by state action.

Wealth is created through private effot. Through the combination of land, labor, capital, management and creativity, we build, make, and grow all that creates wealth. In the process, we create jobs, raise living standards, and empower all to rise to their interests and abilities. Government does not create jobs or wealth; it grows nothing (*except debt*), it makes nothing (*except laws and regulations*) and it builds nothing (*except its own expansion*).

Government, of course, is not without value or necessity. Its value is in doing those things that, by virtue of sheer scale, necessity, or lack of profit incentive, need to be done for the general welfare of its citizens (not the special interests). Its necessity is in protecting the nation and maintaining peace and international relations. These purposes are limited and constitutionally defined. A friend of mine once remarked accurately, *"If you can find it in the yellow pages, the government shouldn't be doing it."* That pretty well sums it up.

People naturally act in their self-interest; they are motivated by profit. They profit from their labor, their investment, their property, and their creative ability. Their objective is the attainment and preservation of their basic human needs. It is through the business enterprise - whether self-employed, small business, or corporation - that financial gain is acquired. Financial gain is, in fact, the only purpose of the business enterprise. When basic needs are met, an individual is free to explore a higher purpose, as a matter of choice and personal moral principle, not government requirements or corporate squandering.

Competition is an essential component of capitalism. The existence of many small, competing interests is what fosters efficiency, innovation, and productivity. While economies of scale are achieved as an enterprise grows, there is a point at which bureaucracy replaces efficiency; innovation is stifled in favor of corporate politics; and productivity falls as a result of excess regulation and unionization.

Competition needs to be reinvented periodically, however. Success breeds growth, and growth breeds economic power and further success. Government actions (and inactions) can aid the process. By permitting unrestrained mergers and acquisitions, rapid growth is accommodated. By creation of complex regulations and taxation preferences, large organizations are often favored. A kind of economic Darwinism occurs and oligopoly replaces broad competition. In fact, most every major industry and service sector in our economy today is dominated by 5 or fewer companies controlling 70-80% of market share. *That is not competition.*

Free markets are required for capitalism to exist. The existence of many competing firms requires ease of entry into markets. Entry is facilitated by low regulation, low taxation, access to capital, legal protection of ideas, and parity in international trade. Free markets are hindered when government subsidies favor one enterprise over another, when taxes and regulation are burdensome, and when consumer's choices are mandated rather than freely made. The public is being forced into accepting windmill and solar farms, for example, when it would likely not support them if the full cost were paid directly; they only exist because they are heavily subsidized. They become viable only because a significant cost of energy production is buried in taxation rather than levied directly as a product cost.

An unrestrained labor force is required for capitalism to function. An individual controls the choice of where to market his or her labor and on what terms. Mandatory union membership and excessive union control limits, rather than protects, worker choices. The results, as can be seen in the automotive and education fields, are disastrous when choice is usurped from the individual by the collective organization. Wages and benefits are no longer allowed to reach equilibrium between supply and demand, but are instead artificially manipulated.

Capitalism is governed by the natural relationship of supply and demand. Where demand for products and services exist, businesses will spring up to meet that demand. If consumer attitudes shift, demand will wane and those businesses will adjust or cease to exist. Government bailouts and subsidies of unsuccessful businesses fly in the face of normal economics, and preserve outdated, inefficient, or even dysfunctional organizations – often simply because of political favor. Government regulation mandating production of one type of product or otherwise directing consumer behavior by force rather than choice is a recipe for disaster.

For consumers to act rationally, they must be fully informed. The goal of perfect information is likely unattainable, but it is certainly diminished when government – not sellers – is the source of that information and the goal is indoctrination rather than enlightenment. Information about energy and "global warming" is far from consistent yet government advocates attempt to promote an agenda driven by politics rather than provide accurate information from *all* sources.

There is a legitimate public role in capitalism but it is not the one being played. It does not force consumer behavior; it does not prop up failed or unproven ideas or companies; it does not create jobs or wealth. In fact, it does nothing that unfettered capitalism cannot do better left to its natural state.

The legitimate role of government is to foster capitalism by breaking up companies when they become so successful that they become monopolies or oligopolies, usually through successive mergers, acquisitions, and sheer financial dominance, not superiority in the free market.

A legitimate role of government is to establish and maintain natural monopolies, where justified, as public utilities. Systems *infrastructure* essential to transportation, telecommunications, and energy delivery are examples. Government should yield to private enterprise, however, when the latter can perform the job better, such as energy exploration and production and the manufacture of automobiles and telecommunication products.

A legitimate role of government is to provide those goods and services for which there is demand and constitutional authority, but insufficient profit potential to attract private investment. It is not to provide those things not within its constitutional authority; that is, for special interests rather than the general welfare of the citizenry.

A legitimate role of government is to regulate for the health and safety of the public, but with the reasonable expectation of consumers to be informed and reasonably responsible for their choices. Regulation should be minimal, directed, and essential. Government has long since departed from this standard. Today, regulation is so onerous that it severely limits entry into markets and is probably the single biggest impediment to the functioning of capitalism. Consider just *some* of the laws dealing with employment issues:

• American with Disabilities Act (ADA) (protection of disabled citizens)
• Child Labor Laws (hiring and pay of minors)
• Employee Law -- Civil Rights Act of 1964 (the major act of Congress which started many employee laws)
• Consolidated Omnibus Reconciliation Act (COBRA) (continuation of health benefits)

• Health Insurance Portability and Accountability Act (HIPAA) (health insurance coverage)
• Eligibility of Alien Workers in the U.S.
• Employee Retirement Income Security Act (ERISA) (protects against misuse of benefit plans)
• Fair Labor Standards Act (FLSA) (compensation, exempt and nonexempt, overtime, etc.)
• Family and Medical Leave Act (FMLA)|Family and Medical Leave Act (FMLA) (job-protected leave for medical emergencies)]
• Federal Employee Compensation Act (FECA) (Worker's Compensation) (injured workers)
• Occupational Safety and Health Administration Act (OSHA) (safety in the workplace)
• Unemployment Compensation (benefits to qualified, unemployed workers seeking work)
• Uniformed Services Employment and Reemployment Rights Act (USERRA)

What entrepreneur would start a new business in such a maze of regulatory insanity?

As the government embarks down a path of socialism and incredible spending under the guise of economic "stimulus," it is well worth considering that the failure in our economy is traceable to just one thing: *the demise of capitalism.* We have allowed companies to become "too big to fail," rather than break them up into smaller, efficient, and innovative organizations. We have allowed companies to become so large and distant from shareholders that obscene compensation and executive perks have become ordinary. We have exported most of our manufacturing capacity and millions of jobs to foreign competitors by signing trade agreements without market parity. We have allowed big labor to supercede market forces and shut down industries or make them incompetent. We have regulated to death most every industry with either general or targeted regulations. We have used taxation as a bludgeon for compliance with social engineering goals rather than profit and success. We have interfered with normal market mechanisms by subsidizing and rewarding special interests. We have justified interference in the marketplace based on political contributions and favoritism, rather than economic superiority.

And now, we are being sold the illusion that only government can fix the economy and create jobs – to the tune of perhaps $10,000,000,000,000... count the zeros. This is anything but capitalism.

"Great nations are never impoverished by private, though they sometimes are by public prodigality and misconduct. The whole, or almost the whole public revenue, is in most countries employed in maintaining unproductive hands... Such people, as they them-selves produce nothing, are all maintained by the produce of other men's labour... Those unproductive hands, who should be maintained by a part only of the spare revenue of the people, may consume so great a share of their whole revenue, and thereby oblige so great a number to encroach upon their capitals, upon the funds destined for the maintenance of productive labour, that all the frugality and good conduct of individuals may not be able to compensate the waste and degradation of produce occasioned by this violent and forced encroachment."
~ Adam Smith, The Wealth of Nations, Book II, Chapter III

§

FAILED SYSTEMS
Health

"Government health care changes the relationship between the citizen and the state, and, in fact, I think it's an assault on citizenship."
~ Mark Steyn

HEALTH CARE
The patient is sick, not dead *(OCT 2009)*

The problem with the current debate on health care is that it is not about health care at all; *it is about yet another transfer of power from the citizen to the state.* From the perspective of the citizens, that reality is reaching the boiling point. The "tea parties" were, and are, misperceived as being about taxes. They aren't. They are about the frustration citizens feel about an over-reaching, abusive, intrusive, and tyrannical government. Taxation is only a part of the equation. In the same manner, explosive town hall meetings are revealing similar frustration; this time, on the heels of the health care debate. It's about health care - but it is much more.

Two things are certain regarding health care in the U.S. One, the system is far from broken. Two, a take-over by the federal government is not the way to fix it even if it were.

History has shown us that the solution to any societal problem, real or imagined, is not to be found in a single, grand piece of "reform" legislation. It should be clear that answers should come from health and medical professionals, not politicians and bureaucrats. It should also be clear from common sense that needs and abilities are different for different people. And it should be very clear that 1,100 pages of legalese and 500 amendments promoted by special interests are only going to compound a complex situation and add to the problem. The solutions will not, and should not, come quickly, contrary to the demands of the Obama administration and the Democrats controlling Congress.

Why Americans aren't buying "health care reform."
The American people don't want another vast, federal bureaucracy guided by thousands of pages of regulations, driven by partisan politics and special interests, and run by mindless bureaucrats. They don't want another excuse for excessive taxation, government mandates on behavior, and control over personal decisions.

Americans don't want yet another national program catering to trial attorneys or special interests, and supporting the needs of illegal immigrants. They don't really care what the AMA, AARP and ACORN think; they are tired of big, and often corrupt, lobbying interests pushing their own self-serving agendas.

Americans don't want another government program so wonderful that Congress exempts itself and public employees from it. They want government to clean up the messes it has already made, and pursue the waste, fraud, and corruption that currently plague its former creations. Americans don't want health care becoming the next "General Motors."

What Americans do want in health care.
The following are among the possible improvements that do not require a massive, national government intervention or take-over. Neither do they require a trillion dollars of new spending. Many, in fact, will reduce spending. Here they are:

Education Reforms
• Require P.E., health and hygiene classes in all K-12 educational programs. Create a federal guide as a *model* for states, not a federal program. Educate for healthy living.
• Require proof of citizenship, immunization and health status for enrollment in schools at all levels.
• Increase availability of medical education facilities and encourage the

entry into health related fields. Restore the prestige, honor and rewards accorded to those serving in health and medical fields. Promote scholarships, public and private, based on service in military, VA, free/rural clinics, and other public service facilities assisting seniors, veterans and the poor.

Patient Reforms
• Require personal responsibility for basic and reasonably anticipated costs, including office visits and co-pays. If patients want more, they can buy more via insurance. Accept that treatment will not be equal; if someone pays more, they will get more. *Life's not fair.*
• Promote development of individual and small business co-ops for pooled negotiations, insurance, pre-paid medical and other cost savings systems.

Legal Reforms
• Cap medical malpractice awards based on "pain and suffering." *Nothing in life is perfect, nor should it be expected to be.*
• Establish state malpractice panels to review all malpractice claims and promote arbitration as an alternative to litigation. Permit panel and arbitration data and conclusions to be included in any subsequent litigation. Make nuisance litigants pay for trial costs.
• Permit discounts by health providers for waiver of legal liability by patients. Allow patients who trust their doctors more than their lawyers the benefit of removing litigation from the health cost equation.

Doctor-Patient Reforms
• Encourage computerization of records and integration with hospital, pharmacy and related medical products and services. This can be a private system. Citizens *must* have the option to exclude themselves from any public/government database. Assign a unique medical ID and disallow the use of social security numbers for further privacy protection.
• Restore dignity and professionalism to doctor-patient relationships by excluding government, not allowing it greater intrusion.
• Stop trying to control the incomes of doctors and other medical professionals. We don't control that of lawyers, rap singers or baseball players - why doctors and nurses, of all people?

Hospital Reforms
• Provide incentives for community and regional hospitals to be run as non-profit organizations, and require patient and insurance billing to be based on the same costs. The cost of patient care should be the same whether paid for by the patient, an insurance company, or a government agency - there is no equitable justification for volume discounting!
• Deal with the poor by encouraging the development of privately or publicly subsidized facilities such as the Shriner's and St. Jude's, VA, county hospitals, and free/low cost clinics. Prevent high-cost emergency rooms from being used as medical clinics.

Insurance Reforms
• Increase competition by allowing purchase of insurance across state lines.
• Prohibit rejection based on existing claims or pre-existing conditions. Allow rating differential to a maximum of plus or minus 20% to reflect health, lifestyle, or medical conditions.
• Do not set coverage requirements, but encourage a variety of plain-language coverage options to meet the needs of different age and health level groups. Let the marketplace respond to what consumers want, not government mandates.

Pharmaceutical Reforms
• Prohibit the sale of pharmaceuticals for more than 20% higher than the lowest price charged worldwide. *Stop subsidizing Canada and other Socialist medical systems.*
• Streamline the FDA approval process and intellectual property protection; place caps on liability for approved products.
• Allow generic products upon recovery of drug development expenses.

Tax Reforms
• Stop using the tax system to punish and reward. Make all insurance, medical costs, and medical savings accounts exempt from all taxes. *The cost of preserving the health of oneself or one's family should not be bonus to government.*

Government Reforms
• Set up state commissions to analyze methods for improved operation of Medicare/Medicaid and VA systems. Commissions should be comprised of medical professionals, health educators, hospital management, pharmaceutical and medical equipment manufacturers, and citizens. Establish national non-profit clearinghouses to annually review and discuss state experiences for possible adoption by other states and federal government. *Let the private sector compete, innovate, imagine, and invent.*

Don't tread on us
Americans are getting fed up with a government that seeks to manage and control every aspect of their lives. They have had it with vast expansion of the domain of the national government to areas in which it has no expertise, no constitutional authority, and no business. The incremental approach to tyrannical control used for decades has been accelerated under this president and this Congress to allow a take-over of the auto industry, the banking and finance industry, the securities industry, and the economy as a whole.

An attempt to effect "Marshall Law" over health care will not be tolerated. Together with a Machiavellian desire to take over the Internet and free speech in radio and cable news, this power grab may well be the fuel necessary to spark the next American Revolution. The egoists in Washington D.C. don't seem to get it. The American people do.

"If 'Obamanation' health care goes through, I'm going to Belize and opening a 'wine and pap' shop.
  - Heather Thomas, OB-GYN Nurse Practitioner

§

FAILED SYSTEMS
Taxation

"For imposing Taxes on us without our Consent.... We, therefore... solemnly publish and declare, That these United Colonies are, and of Right ought to be Free and Independent States."
   ~ The Declaration of Independence of the Thirteen Colonies

THE INCOME TAX
An abomination to liberty *(APR 2009)*

In 1913, we allowed the seeds to be sown for the greatest violation of our liberties since our separation from England 130 years earlier with the passage of the 16th Amendment to the Constitution: *the income tax.*

This monumental blunder gave to our government virtually unlimited and unchecked power to take, not just our money, but our freedom. As will be seen, it was much more than a means of securing revenue for the legitimate needs of government; it was the most successful tool of tyranny ever devised.

The Framers of the Constitution were aware of the power inherent in the ability to tax. They addressed that issue by specifically limiting the role of government and by limiting taxation primarily to consumption taxes. Section 8 of the Constitution provided that: *"The Congress shall have Power To lay and collect Taxes, Duties, Imposts and Excises, to pay the Debts and provide for the common Defence and general Welfare of the United States; but all Duties, Imposts and Excises shall be uniform throughout the United States."* An impost was a tax on imported goods, while an excise was simply a sales tax; a tax on consumption. The

General Welfare referred, of course, to the happiness and prosperity of *all* Americans, not various special interests.

That was all changed with the 16th Amendment which provided the broad, unlimited power to take from Americans, without need, justification, or consent; *"The Congress shall have power to lay and collect taxes on incomes, from whatever source derived, without apportionment among the several States, and without regard to any census or enumeration."*

An income tax was adopted on two occasions prior to the 16th Amendment. In 1862, during the Civil War, a progressive income tax was adopted with rates of 3-10%. It was repealed in 1872 but revived again in 1894, only to be ruled unconstitutional. The Constitution was, of course, amended and in 1913 the income tax was made permanent, with a top rate of 7%. Supreme Court Justice Stephen J. Field ominouosly predicted that the small progressive tax *"will become the stepping stone to others, larger and more sweeping, till our political contests will become a war of the poor against the rich."* How right he was. Like most onerous political actions, this was to start out as limited and innocuous, only to be slowly and incrementally ratcheted up until the intended total effect was achieved.

Rates would be raised at the whims of politicians, and in 1941 President Roosevelt proposed a top rate of 99.5%. He actually issued an executive order levying a rate of 100% on incomes over $25,000, which was later reduced by Congress to 90%. In decades to follow, there would be a string of abuses, misuses, punishments, and rewards tied to the income tax. The "beast" would grow to over 70,000 pages of inane regulations with an estimated 6 million words understood by no one. The cost of complying with this monstrosity would grow to $300 billion or more each year.

The income tax is an immoral, insane, and despotic abuse for which the Founders of our country would never have stood. The Boston Tea Party and revolt against the Stamp Act were reactions to relatively mild attempts to unfairly tax the colonists. Think what the reaction to the modern day income tax would have been. Public officials would have been tarred and feathered, and run out of town. The issues of taxes and freedom became the foundation, in fact, for the American evolution. Today we have come to accept this travesty and abuse of power as tolerable. *It was not then, it is not now, and it never will be.*

The income tax is uncontrollable by the citizens, as a consumption tax was expected to be. If citizens felt abused by taxation under a consumption tax, they could simply stop spending. Not so with a tax on one's labor or investments; if you work or profit, you pay. Even the Constitution offers no restraint to spending when it is ignored by government which takes and spends as it sees fit. Government is not constrained to spend for the "general welfare," nor for its own specific and limited purposes as defined. No, it gives the citizen's money to foreign countries, corporations, factions, special interest groups, and all manner of causes for which it has no authority to give.

The income tax is used to reward political friends and punish political enemies. Tax provisions are enacted regularly, which lessen the burden on favored groups or individuals. Social engineering agendas are advanced through tax "policy" to favor "desired" behaviors, while punishing "undesirable" ones. Some companies or industries are rewarded with subsidies, while others are punished. There is no equality in taxation, there is no reason; there is only political motivation and personal interest serving those who make the rules.

Having more children than one can afford is encouraged by tax policies, as is buying a house beyond one's means. Saving is not. Being inefficient, ineffective, lazy, or even a failure is rewarded. Being successful is punished. Being a perpetual student can yield special tax treatment. Learning a trade and working just permits you to pay more.

Financial decisions are often made for "tax reasons," not for economic motivations. Individuals and companies alike are encouraged to do things which might be considered stupid, were it not for some tax incentive. The same money is taxed twice, three times, or more. A corporation is taxed on earnings, then the same money is taxed again as distributions to share-holders who are taxed yet again when they spend the money or make additional earnings from investments. "Paper profits," never realized, can result in tax obligations, while real monetary losses are often ignored.

The privacy of citizens is invaded with information demanded about all manner of expenses and payments which is not the business of the government to know. Citizens are asked to sign forms under penalty of perjury, and then given rules so complex that perjury is all but assured in the attempt for compliance. Information obtained in the tax process may be viewed by politicians as a means of embarrassing, punishing, or even blackmailing their political enemies, while friends may receive special treatment. Richard Nixon, in describing his desired IRS commissioner, said, *"I want to be sure that he is ...ruthless ...that he will do what he is told, that every income-tax return I want to see, I see. That he will go after our enemies and not go after our friends. It is as simple as that."* Hillary Clinton had 200 tax folders *somehow* show up on her desk while her husband was president. The system is filled with potential for mischief and evil.

It's clear why politicians refuse to scrap the current system: it is to their immense self-interest to keep it in place. They and they alone have the power to use the income tax system for their benefit; to punish and reward, to encourage contributions, to gain personally, and to remain in power. That is the bottom line.

There will be "tea parties" held around the country on April 15th. While these are symbolic events, recalling the Boston Tea Party, they are much more. They are evidence of the growing anger and frustration by the citizens that the tax system is an abuse and must be replaced. They are a harbinger of greater anger and frustration to come if Congress and the president fail to act. Just as King George III dismissed the event in Boston Harbor, our arrogant political class will dismiss these. They are making a big mistake. Revolution followed the protests of 1776, and that response is available to the citizens still. Time, however, is running out.

An alternative to the income tax has been developed and has many advantages. While the "Fair Tax" not perfect, it is a vast improvement over the present system. In addition to repealing the 16th amendment, it would rid us of the IRS and place collections in the form of a single sales tax at the state level. It, or something similar, should be adopted immediately, and followed by a similar measure at the state level to rid us of all other onerous income taxes and regulations.

"There is no method of steering clear of this inconvenience, but by authorizing the national government to raise its own revenues in its own way. Imposts, excises, and, in general, all duties upon articles of consumption, may be compared to a fluid, which will, in time, find its level with the means of paying them. The amount to be contributed by each citizen will in a degree be at his own option, and can be regulated by an attention to his resources. The rich may be extravagant, the poor can be frugal; and private oppression may always be avoided by a judicious selection of objects proper for such impositions. ... It is a singular advantage of taxes on articles of consumption that they contain in their own nature a security against excess. They prescribe their own limit, which cannot be exceeded without defeating the end purposed - that is, an extension of the revenue."

~ Alexander Hamilton, Federalist No. 21

§

CHAPTER 5

VALUES AND CULTURE

All animals are equal, but some are more equal than others.
- George Orwell, "Animal Farm"

PROTECTED CLASSES
We are NOT all equal *(APR 2007)*

It is essential, in advancing the philosophy of the Left, to have victims. After all, if we are truly created equal, or even rise to a level of equality, what need is there for government programs and protections. And government expansion is the ultimate goal of Liberals, Progressives and Statists. There is no room for individual thinking, action, or responsibility – only the collective contribution shouldered by a willing super-nanny: *government.*

There is no need for reality in victimhood. Victims are politically defined as a matter of purpose and convenience. As such, race is a defining characteristic; so is sex. The problem is, some races don't fit the defined victim minority profile, and women – classic victims – are generally a *majority.* Hispanics, and Mexicans specifically, comprise a politically convenient victim class but they are Caucasian. As such, the race distinction can't apply – so we broaden the test from race to ethnicity or nationality…at least for some. Mexicans are a protected class, but Spaniards are not. Asians, a racial minority in many areas, have no problem learning English quickly, adopting American cultural values, and achieving in many academic fields, notably science and engineering. Those traits do not bode well for victim status!

Note the flexibility in determining inequality or unfair advantage. There is no logic or reason; it is a creation of the mind, or rather the mind of those who benefit most by the perpetuation of protected classes: *politicians.*

Slavery – the 1st sin

Never mind that slavery existed in some form in most cultures at the time of our own engagement in the abominable practice. Never mind that the practice was abolished at the expense of a civil war during which over half a million – mostly white – died. Never mind that no one currently living directly supported slavery or was directly enslaved. Never mind that despite trillions of dollars spent in racially targeted social programs, there are still claims of unfairness to black descendants of slaves. Where does it end? It doesn't. The existence of inequality among blacks is essential to the mission of the Left.

Voting rights – the 2nd sin

The end of voting discrimination against women came in 1920. That in no way ended the ability of politicians and special interest groups to invent an inequality for women. They are still trying to legitimize the unequal standing of women by pushing the Equal Rights Amendment – a process that started in 1972. This, despite the hard reality that the Constitution does not limit the entitlement of ANY rights to citizens on the basis of their sex; *they already have equal rights!* Radical "women's rights" organizations are a staple of the Left, however, so perpetuating the notion of woman as second class citizens is essential to their existence. Are women really left out? Let's consider the experience of Carson City, Nevada - a not untypical city in America. Carson City has a female city manager, a female Chamber of Commerce executive director, a female college president, and a female superintendent of schools… hmmm.

The momentum of guilt

A sense of guilt goes a long way in advancing a cause. As such, MADD mothers legitimately grieving over the loss of loved ones are portrayed as sufferers, justifying the passage of stricter laws that penalize NOT the causation of harm, but the mere potential to do so. Why is that same standard not applied to, say, carriers of AIDS?

Does the tragic loss by families of those killed on 9/11 justify the millions of public dollars awarded to them, when other tragic losses are uncompensated:

a child drowing in a pool; an auto accident victim; even a soldier killied in action. Does the holocaust horror against Jews justify bending over backward to not offend Muslims, though many among them have committed to Jihad against us? Guilt is a wonderful tool in justifying inequality – making some more equal than others.

The reality of politics

Why are homosexuals, illegal immigrants, certain races, seniors, and the disabled given special standing at the expense of others? Why are they given special standing, instead of equal standing? The answer is simple - they tend to vote as a block based on a single ideological point: their special status. That status confers upon them special benefits, which perpetuates them as "unequal." The philosophy of the Liberal Left is based on this reality. Those on the Left require inequality to carry out their agenda – even if they have to invent it.

Exceptions

Sometimes inequality is revealed in special treatment. In sexual assault crimes, for example (consider the Duke Lacrosse team case), the accuser is accorded privacy and protection from revealing past sexual proclivities and excesses. The accused are publicly identified and dragged through the mud on mere accusation.

Sometimes, inequality relies on facts which benefit the "cause" while ignoring those which conflict with it. In professional sports, there is no shortage of stories on the inequality by race among team owners, coaches and managers. There is nothing said, however, about the huge inequality in the percentage of highly paid (generally black) athletes. White business executives are regularly pummeled for excessive compensation, but little mention is made of black, Hispanic, female or gay celebrities raking in millions.

Promoting the cause

Hate crimes legislation has been passed in many states and is currently being pushed at the federal level. In reality, the same crime committed against two different individuals is still the same crime. That is, unless, there is a benefit to ruling it otherwise. Thus, the murder of a gay person is worth more politically than to simply bundle it up with the murders of all others. This is one way the cause of inequality is perpetuated.

Take this challenge: Watch television for an evening and see how many black and other minority actors appear in commercials. Typically, you will see 50-60 percent, this despite the reality that blacks compromise 11-12% of the population. Why is this? *Propaganda.* Simply showcasing black individuals disproportionately draws attention to their "special class" standing; a sort of a "reverse psychology" approach to controlling your mind. It also soothes the guilt of Hollywood Liberals who continue to think blacks and others in "protected classes" are denied access to opportunity.

In education, tactics are more bold and controlling. The lessons being foisted upon young impressionable minds are clear: America is bad (war mongers and rich), poor countries are good (struggling and happy); straights are bad (homophobic), gays are good (just an alternative lifestyle); whites are bad (colonial slave owners); blacks are good (oppressed and struggling); legitimate citizens are bad (anti-immigrant); Illegals are good (doing the work Americans won't do)… and so on.

Thus, despite the pronouncement of our Declaration of Independence, we are not – in fact – all equal. We are very much unequal – and it is in the best interest of politics, as we know it, to preserve that fantasy forever. God bless us everyone – no matter how unequal we may be.

"From each according to his abilities, to each according to his needs."
    ~ Karl Marx and Frederick Engels
    The Communist Manifesto

§

MORAL RELATIVISM (DEC 2002)

"We must take human nature as we find it, perfection falls not to the share of mortals."
~ *George Washington*

Human behavior is different from all others in that it involves reasoned moral options - choosing between right and wrong. It is not simply instinctive. It includes rational consideration of the act, or inaction, itself, as well as a consideration of outcomes and consequences. Moral behavior is reinforced by social rules that define the nature of acceptable conduct between individuals and entities for the design and operation of civilization. Such rules may be present as personal guides, where compliance is motivated simply by the individual's desire for good, or codified into law, with punishment for failure to conform.

Moral relativism, or "situation ethics," is the belief that concepts such as right and wrong, goodness and badness, or truth and falsehood are not absolute but can and do vary from culture to culture and situation to situation. There is, of course, a "gray area" where uncertainty is legitimate, but the "gray" has expanded to the point where one is prompted to ask, "Whatever happened to right and wrong?"

Norms and Values
The Relativists are right on at least one thing: morality does vary from culture to culture. This is why a common culture is fundamental to any civilization; even more so for a sovereign state which is granted the right and responsibility to create laws by which it and its citizens operate. When the norms and values of such a sovereign culture are diluted or removed, moral confusion is bound to arise.

Our American culture is derived from a Christian ethic reflected in the Ten Commandments; it has largely Western European origins and includes English as its native language. Our moral code is based on western civilization, including its legal system and institutions, and acknowledgement of fundamental laws of nature. Our values support individual freedom and responsibility; encourage tolerance of differing views; and celebrate the diversity of the world around it, in all manners consistent with and not detrimental to our fundamental nature. It is in this last area that many problems have arisen. There are, in fact, many who see nothing wrong with the undermining of our culture, or even the intentional subversion of it for some other end. In their actions, they have "grayed" morality so that right and wrong are no longer seen as clear choices.

We have always been tolerant of ideas foreign to the mainstream, with freedom to dissent enshrined in our Constitution. Political correctness, however, has made some tolerance mandatory, even as it destroys our basic values, while other forms are rejected. The modern mantra is, "Who am I to judge?" This question fails to distinguish between judging the individual and judging the behavior. In fact, that imbalance frequently plays into the hands of political correctness. A gun owner or member of the NRA is judged as evil, while the use of a gun with evil intent or consequences is often explained away (mentally incompetent, young, victim of taunting, etc.). The same logic twisting is used to condemn as "homophobes" the vast majority that consider homosexual behavior wrong, though not judging the individual. In fact, such a distinction between the behavior and the individual is not only proper, but also necessary, if a society is to have norms at all.

"Diversity" is used to undermine values when it is viewed as a justification rather than a condition. It takes the value of equality and perverts it, justifying special preferences for some, even on goals carefully constructed to meet a particular end. Business, government, and major institutions have all been swayed into this politically correct mind-set, further eroding the concept of right and wrong. Our schools make some religions and cultures required areas of study, while ignoring, even prohibiting, those fundamental to our own historical culture. Some would punish programs such as the Boy Scouts for asserting basic norms such as heterosexuality, while facilitating programs promoting needle exchange and abortion.

Clearly norms and values are the basis for right and wrong, and clearly the traditional norms and values upon which our country is based are under attack. There is a war being waged from within, and it is not simply due to terrorism.

Laws
The vehicle for measuring and controlling moral behavior is our system of laws. So why don't they work? Compare the Ten Commandments or the "Golden Rule" to our system of laws. The former are simple, reasoned and succinct, while our laws are too often complex, arcane and run millions of pages of verbose text. Our norms and values – right and wrong – are collapsing under the sheer weight of the excesses to micro-manage them! Albert Einstein once remarked, *"The solutions to problems should be as simple as possible, but no more."* Our legislatures at all levels have failed terribly in meeting this standard.

Consider the simple but elegant language of the Mayflower Compact, Articles of Confederation, Declaration of Independence, and the Constitution. In these relatively brief documents, our culture and basic rights were defined, our posterity protected, and our country established. Over 200 years, it is arguable as to whether we have improved or severely diminished the effectiveness of those documents in defining right and wrong.

Discomfort and Punishment
Since our laws define moral behavior, at least in theory; our systems of punishment should encourage compliance with them and discourage or penalize departure from them. We have sadly reached a point where they do neither. Why?

In an earlier time, a pregnant teen would have been expected to leave school to have her child, and the father (who was more likely to be known) to find a job to support his new family. There was a stigma attached to the "wrong" behavior and a requirement to do the "right" thing to move forward. Today, the pregnant teen would be celebrated as prom queen and the young dad's primary duty would be guiding his football team to victory. No stigma. No ostracism. No right or wrong – only *misfortune* (and more government programs). Stigma used to be a relatively mild but effective deterrent to wrong behavior; now it's a violation of civil rights.

Callous disregard of society's rules is dealt more serious punishment, in an effort to deter or correct and prevent a reoccurrence. But does it? Criminals are allowed to accumulate mile long rap sheets with continued indulgence. There is greater concern for the comfort of prisoners of war than for the military who risk their lives in guarding them. Terrorists are given high profile legal counsel to assure their rights while average citizens get the public defender (or lose their life savings.) A criminal injured in the process of committing a crime is awarded damages by our "justice" system. Laws are written to generate revenue for government rather than to deal with crime. For Hollywood and corporate celebrities, politicians, or those simply wealthy, there is community service – or even purchased "innocence."

It gets even better for our worst offenders. If they are not exonerated as mentally incompetent, youthful offenders, or victims of society, they may actually be sent to prison. Unlike so many law-abiding citizens who work and struggle, violent criminals receive food, clothing, shelter, and quality medical care (even heart transplants) as a right. There are libraries and gyms, organized sports, and recreation. In recent months, we have seen violent offenders featured on Viacom's VH-1 television as "rock stars." Just how ridiculous can it get? The tragedy is that we are not talking about relatively minor or non-violent offenders. These are violent criminals who have severely violated or ended the lives of other innocent people, or caused massive harm to lives and property.

Moral Leadership

It's clear we have problems. So where is the moral leadership? We have defenses of moral failing like "it depends on what the meaning of 'is' is," or "there is no controlling legal authority." Sadly there appears no more personal sense of guilt and responsibility than there is public. Remorse, guilt, and humility are apparently not becoming to public figures. Bill Clinton's outrageous pardons of criminals caused hardly a ripple of concern among other leaders; there was simply no "proof" of a quid pro quo. The convenient timing of Hillary's book deal was tossed off as just good fortune, kind of like her trading in the commodities market. The Democrat Party has no problem with violating laws to get elected, inventing dubious means of divining intentions from a "hanging chad," or using any other extreme that is not "technically" wrong. The Republicans are often no better. The list goes on and on – *and this is leadership?*

How about our religious leaders? Surely they would exemplify moral behavior unvarnished by convenient interpretations. What we see, however, is commercial TV evangelism focused more on money than morality. Jesse Jackson has built an empire on tactics of racial division and questionable coercive practices. The Catholic Church has serious and divisive problems with homosexual behavior in conflict with its basic tenets, and worse, afflicted with seemingly unending acts of sexual abuse. A lack of strong and effective leadership from the church on this issue is damaging to the concept of right and wrong far beyond church corridors.

Entertainment and sports celebrities are not expected to be role models for moral behavior, and they generally don't let us down. Lesbian and single parent adoptions are common, much like acquiring a new trinket. Michael Jackson showed off his parenting skills recently by dangling his infant child over a hotel balcony. Others merely hire a nanny to fill in for things they can't accommodate – *like childhood.* Then there are the routine drugs, shoplifting, and spousal abuse that go hand and hand with the celebrity culture. As excess goes farther and farther down the tubes, the standard for comparison – *the norm* - is degraded along with it.

Our families, as noted in a previous article, have been in disarray for several decades, with dysfunction becoming the rule. How can the family provide moral leadership when it either doesn't exist at all, or is intrinsically unstable and irresponsible? Parents who are there and do care still need to compete with the "values" of movies, music, and television that are often greatly at odds with their own. When the foul-mouthed youth "star" Eminem produces a movie that actually sells, it's sad. When his movie is a hit, it's a tragic example of how far down family values have fallen. When a mom or dad takes their 11-year kid to see it, it borders on child abuse. Yet, that is exactly what is happening with many families today. Schools don't help much with an NEA agenda that ranges from anti-American to downright sick. Far too many corporations care more about sales no matter how sleazy the advertising message. Families that care feel helpless; those that don't continue to drag new generations of children into the muck with them.

Material Choices

Money may not be the root of all evil, but the focus on the material at the expense of the moral is evident in all segments of our society. We have leadership at the highest levels pandering, even endangering national security, for money.

People used to enter government, civil or political, and we called it public service. Today it is simply an overpaid, unionized job with more holidays, larger paychecks, and less concern with what is right than "what's in it for me." There is plenty of avarice in the private sector too, where even the idealism of youth often succumbs to the "big bucks, easy money" route. Hard work, diligence, honesty, integrity, and loyalty all seem rather old fashioned. That isn't to suggest that material rewards for performance are bad. The centerpiece of our capitalist tradition is the system of reward for achievement and results. But when money becomes the *objective* rather than the *reward*, the end of service becomes disconnected, and right and wrong once more become blurred.

The "greatest generation" of WWII Vets came home after sacrificing to make the world a safe place and didn't need much: a three bedroom (often one bath) house, a family car (generally used), a decent job, dinner with the family, and an education for their kids. By contrast, so many today seem *less* content living in million dollar homes large enough to house three families, driving a couple of BMWs, and working for other "things" so much that they have no time for family. They have gone beyond capitalism, and moved on to greed and a do-whatever-it-takes mode of integrity.

So is all lost? Hardly. There was a great story told a while back about a Fuller Brush salesman named Bill Porter. It's an incredible story of a man who, despite the great physical burdens of his cerebral palsy, gets himself up and walks – *walks* – the tortuous miles of his route each day with a smile; doing the right thing for himself and for the world around him. It's a heartwarming example of one man with lots of reasons for taking the easy road but instead, taking the high road - *because it's right.*

Then there was the manufacturer who suffered a plant fire that put his company out of business for two years. Unlike the "leadership" of Enron, Global Crossing and too many others, he took the morally correct path. He continued to pay his employees for the entire period - every one of them. He didn't have to, he just did. There wasn't a union coercing him, or a call for more laws to make him, or even a plea for the government to bail him out. When reminded he had no legal obligation and asked why he did it, he replied: *"because it was the right thing to do."*

Responsibility
When responsibility for moral actions is diminished, so is the tendency to act morally. We live in an era where we punish the many for the acts of the few. Civil liberties in our country are at risk for all citizens because a small number of terrorists have been given the keys to the gates. Why? *Political correctness.* Why don't we do the right thing, and tighten – even shut down – our immigration programs until we get a handle on the problems associated with them? Why don't we infringe more on the liberties of those likely for association with evil than average citizens? Instead, we hassle grandmothers carrying knitting needles on planes. And where are the calls for removal - even punishment - for dereliction by public officials and political leaders who allowed terrorism to take root through their incompetence, or worse, self-serving actions?

A murderer pulls a trigger and kills in cold-blood, and there are screams for gun control, as if the weapon triggered itself. A drunken driver kills through careless and irresponsible behavior, and there are calls for more punitive drinking laws. We punish the instrument rather than the offender. Moral culpability rests with the "carpenter" – not the "tool!"

In supporting a "woman's right to choose," we elevate the *right* of the decision above the consequences of the act. In allowing lawsuits against "deep pocket" defendants we impugn the unwitting bystander, while ignoring the guilty party. Where is the reason, justice, or common sense in punishing the school for a crime committed by a student; for punishing McDonalds for years of indulgence by fat, over-eating kids? Too often, morality is driven by financial considerations, rather than personal responsibility. Culpability gives way to "deep pockets."

Despite the apparent decline in moral behavior, and the expanding "gray zone" promoted by relativism, the vast majority of our citizens are good people. They work hard, do their best, give to others as they can, often in great measure. They feel pain, shame, or remorse when they fall short. Many of our politicians, public employees, heads of businesses, and every day citizens lead lives that are motivated by doing the right thing. None of us is perfect – not the least of whom is this writer, whose short-comings, past and present, are many. It's not easy for any of us. But a basic rule of years past still seems valid today: "If it seems wrong, it probably is." We would all do well to consider that in our daily lives, and hold accountable those who fail to do so.

§

RACE, SEX AND CULTURE (MAR 2008)
Quit Whining

"If the human race wishes to have a prolonged and indefinite period of material prosperity, they have only got to behave in a peaceful and helpful way toward one another."
~ Winston Churchill

Thank you Senator Obama. Thank you for opening the eyes of Americans to what the issue of racism is really about. Thank you Jeremiah Wright, Louis Farrakhan and Jesse Jackson, all Obama supporters, for defining the debate on race in our country. You see, as we have learned from your various pronouncements, the issue is not race, but entitlement and special privilege. Of course, black people are not alone in this convenient interpretation. Many radical feminists, supporters of illegal immigration, homosexuals, and non-Christians are guilty of the same charade. Stop whining and face the truth – and the truth is, whatever historic wrongs may have existed, Americans are the most tolerant, generous, forgiving, and understanding people in history.

Your tactics and claims, Senator, seek not the truth but instead, political accommodation. You have learned one lesson well: spineless politicians will cave in to most any complaint of bias or bigotry and give "things" to those declared victims. Victims will be given money, special protections, special benefits, and special privilege. If they fail, they will blame someone else for their failing. If they are injured, they will characterize the offense as a "hate crime," as if the same crime had different results depending on who the victim is. The charade will play especially well with celebrities, whose disproportion of wealth to societal contribution gives them a special sense of guilt upon which to ply claims of victimization.

THE ISSUE OF RACE
It is suggested by some media pundits that many white people will not vote for Barack Obama simply because he is black; that they are racist.

No one, of course, suggests racism among the more than 90% of black voters who will vote for him *because* he is black. In point of fact, many will not vote for Barack Obama because they believe he is unqualified. They will not vote for him because they believe he proposes a vast social agenda of more government, more taxes, and more infringements on the liberties of Americans. They would feel the same regardless of his race.

Black people comprise 11-12% of the population, yet make up 80% of the National Basketball Association and 65% of the National Football League. Is this because of racism? Hardly. They are simply better athletes proportionally, either naturally gifted or working harder at their craft. No one suggests that they be limited to 11% of the representation in sports, entertainment or other fields in which they predominate. Why then do we speak of racism in business or professions or other areas where blacks are "underrepresented?" Perhaps they are simply less motivated, less qualified by education and experience, or limited by personal choice. In fact, there are black people who excel in all areas of life; it has nothing to do with race, only with achievement.

Why, in fact, do we have Black History Month, Black Entertainment Television, Black Chambers of Commerce and Miss Black America? If there is an exclusionary focus on race in this country it is being driven by blacks and other "minorities." The continued support of these race-based programs is another gift: "looking the other way." If such programs were limited to or promoted by white Americans, they would be pummeled in all circles, and rightly so. The fact is, the issue of race is most often raised by those with a hand out for some special benefit by invoking it.

There are inequalities in life, to be sure. Some are born into broken families, with physical disabilities, with less intelligence, with less athletic ability, or with poor role models. Some are born into stable families, families of wealth, or with physical or mental abilities above the norm. Nothing in our Constitution or way of life guarantees anyone equal results with another; neither does anything, including ones race, preclude the opportunity to pursue happiness on any level or to achieve success. My advice is: work hard, get a good education, pursue excellence in whatever you do - and quit whining.

THE ISSUE OF SEX

Like Obama, Hillary Clinton has made an issue of her "special" status an element in her campaign. There are suggestions that many will not vote for her simply because she is a woman. It is, in fact, their perfectly acceptable right to do so – as is the right of many to vote for her simply because she *is*. In my view, both inclinations are wrong. I will not support Hillary Clinton for many reasons, none of which have anything to do with her gender. I would support a "Maggie Thatcher" in a heartbeat.

Teaching in elementary education is dominated by women. So is nursing. So are many other fields of endeavor. Is that the result of gender bias, or are women just better at doing those things? Perhaps it is simply the fact that fields like elementary education and nursing appeal to the nature of more women, their lifestyle choices, or other factors having nothing to do with their sex *per se*? For whatever reason, why do we not recruit more men for those careers like we beat the drum for more female executives? Note, of course, that no one is beating the drum for more women in the perceptively less cushy jobs of coal miner or garbage man.

Have you heard of Mary Sammons, Anne Mulcahy, Brenda Barnes or Claire Babrowski? They are all CEOs of Fortune 500 companies (Rite Aid, Xerox, Sara Lee, and Radio Shack, respectively). Clearly, while being CEO of a major company statistically favors men, the position is not unattainable by a woman. Again, it is not a matter of a limiting characteristic such as gender; there is no "glass ceiling," except as seen by those who desire special preference.

Politics is no different. Twenty-nine women have been or are currently serving as the governor of a state. There are 16 female senators currently serving and women comprise 16% of the House of Representatives, with Nancy Pelosi as its leader. If a woman is good, and has the desire to do so, she will rise to the top of her field; it's time to stop the whining. (Come to think of it, Nancy Peolosi has demonstrated that a lack of qualification and character isn't even disqualifying!)

THE ISSUE OF CULTURE
Illegal Immigrants

While most illegal immigrants are from Mexico or Latin America and are referred to as "Latino," the designation is not properly a "race." Still, there is a racial overtone – actually one of ethnicity, but the elements are the same. While blacks dwell on the impact of slavery and being taken against their will from their homeland of Africa, Latinos dwell in the accusation that their homeland was taken from them. They too argue that "racism" is at the root of lowered performance achievement. Just as slavery was long ago ended, so have the borders of this country been long established. There has been ample time to move on.

A "racist" or ethnic bias is not the reason Latinos perform less well in education, occupy fewer higher paying jobs, or take up more space in our jails. Their condition is not that different from non-English speaking Asians who, in a generation after coming here, routinely speak English, adopt American culture and values, graduate at the top of their class and occupy high paying positions in business and technology and other fields. Asians, as a whole, simply study and work harder, and their efforts bear the fruit of their choices and family values.

There is no ethnic agenda against Latinos, and white Americans do not hate them. We respect the fact that most of them are hard-working and family centric. We simply demand that they come to this country legally in numbers that can be reasonably accommodated, adopt the language and culture of America, and become either law-abiding residents or citizens. Neither blacks nor Latinos have a claim on reparations, special preferences, aid, accommodation, or treatment – but that is what the race debate is about. It is not about equal treatment; it is about *superior* treatment and a supplanting of our culture and values.

Homosexuals

Homosexuals comprise 1-3% of the population; they are a minority that clearly leads a lifestyle at odds with the cultural norm of our country. Their claims of bias reflect only the fact that they can't have what they want: normalcy and total *acceptance*. It is arrogant to insist that all others accommodate their lifestyle when they refuse to accept that of the vast majority of heterosexuals. There is no "right" to trample the publicly adopted values of the country to promote a behavioral choice that should be left private in the first place. The rejection of homosexual marriage is not a bias against homosexual individuals; it is the preservation of a cultural value that is widely held and of long-standing history.

Pop-culture advocated by the Hollywood crowd and liberal government indoctrination in the education system, continue to coerce the acceptance of homosexuality; its rejection is portrayed as biased and hateful. The fact is, the vast majority of Americans don't hate homosexuals; they simply reject being forced to embrace a lifestyle at odds with views to which *they* themselves are entitled. Tolerance works in both directions.

Religion
America was founded on religious tolerance. That does not confer upon minority religions a special right to forced acceptance or accommodation. The traditions and history of our country are distinctly Christian, not in a religious sense, but in a philosophical one. It is not an affront to celebrate Christian holidays or adopt values and norms based on Christian teachings. That constitutes neither state sponsored religion, nor an unfair bias toward non-Christians; it is simply an acknowledgement of historic facts.

Muslims, Jews and others, unfortunately, demand not tolerance, but an embrace of their religious culture on an equal or even preferred standing. It is not bias or hatred upon which those expectations are rejected, but rather a preservation of our *own* culture.

This is not a Jewish country. This is not a Muslim country. Special accommodation in the public policies or private behavior of citizens is not something to which these groups are entitled. If they come here, it is *they* who must find a way to accommodate their unique religious preferences and requirements. They will be accepted, not catered to. The acceptance of private religious values does not carry with it a public duty to alter that which we are. There is no public duty to accommodate foot washing stations, public prayer, or behaviors that are not consistent with public safety.

SO... Quit Whining

Race, ethnicity, gender and cultural values all affect personal outcomes in life. Such outcomes are not the result of bias by white Americans. If blacks fail to achieve disproportionately to other races, we must look to the failures or poor choices of the individual affected, not blame racism. New immigrants to the country will often start life on the bottom rung of the ladder, as has been the history of millions before them; they can climb the ladder if they choose to. Women have a biological child-bearing and maternal role that is undeniable, but this neither forces nor limits the ability of any woman to follow her choice in any field of endeavor; neither does it assure her success based on some statistically contrived standard of "equality." Values that differ from the historic norms of our country will be tolerated and accepted as personal freedoms, not as an excuse to alter our way of life.

There remains much bias and hatred in our country; it is not being waged by the majority, however, but by various minorities themselves. Their stated objective of acceptance and equality is really a transparent demand for special preference. That politicians, pundits, and pop-culture advocates pander to these demands is not surprising; it is simply wrong. It's time to stand up to these affronts to reason and fairness and stop the intimidation of name-calling. Jeremiah Wright's call for damning America must be rejected with the same fervor he commands from his wrong-headed pulpit. Those who feel put upon in America would do well to stop the finger-pointing and undertake more self-examination and personal responsibility; the duty to make life better is no one's but their own. Of all places on earth, this country excels in fairness and opportunity. *So please ... quit whining.*

§

VIOLENCE (OCT 2006)
What is the proper response?

"An appeaser is one who feeds a crocodile, hoping it will eat him last."
~ Winston Churchill

This past week, the peaceful and simple world of the Amish people of Lancaster County, Pennsylvania was shattered. A small, Protestant sect arriving in the U.S. from Switzerland, they cling to an anachronistic life in a modern world, at the center of which is their faith. That is the tragic irony of it all; that such quiet lives should be interrupted by the inhuman attack of a madman on their children.

Charles Roberts committed such an atrocity, entering a local school and shooting, execution style, 10 little girls ranging in age from 7 to 13. One 13-year-old asked to be killed first in a heroic attempt to perhaps spare the others. Such stoic but tender bravery was extinguished in a crime that defies explanation or understanding; it crushes the soul to even consider what happened that awful day.

So what was the response of the Amish community to this horrific experience? They accepted it as God's will and salved their anguish with grace and forgiveness. They embraced the family of the murderer, as their belief in the teachings of Jesus would compel them to do. How many others could exhibit such poise under those circumstances?

Compare this to the response of Muslims around the world. When Danish cartoons were published mocking their violent nature, they affirmed the characterization by demonstrating violently. When the Pope recently spoke of the need for a dialogue between Christians and Muslims as an alternative to violence, his words were met with more violence, including the killing of a Nun working in a hospital in Somalia. *All because of words!*

So on the one hand, violent atrocities that snuff out the lives of young innocents begets forgiveness, and on the other, words meant to heal beget violence. What is wrong with this picture?

The radical difference in these scenarios is at the heart of much of the violence that permeates the world today. The proper response lies somewhere in between.

This nation, and others, "turned the other cheek" with the attack on the Marine barracks in Beirut, with the hijacking of the Achille Lauro and killing of a wheelchair bound passenger, with the downing of Pan Am flight 103 over Scotland, and with numerous unprovoked attacks and beheadings of innocent journalists and caregivers. All of these attacks have been the actions of young Muslim male extremists.

The difference between the senseless killing of the Amish children and the attack on the World Trade Center defined both the actions of madmen, and the necessary response to their terrible deeds. Both were evil acts; both involved senseless killings of innocents; and both included the suicide-death of the perpetrators as part of their destructive acts. In the first case, however, the act was that of a deranged individual; in the second, the act was a continuing sequence of attacks by a "nation" committed to the annihilation of its sworn "enemies" – Israel, America and the western world.

The amazing acts of grace and forgiveness exhibited by the Amish people are both Christian and noble. But how can an entire civilization turn its collective cheek to the evil visited upon it, which is designed to bring about its extermination? It cannot.

This is the folly of protracted diplomatic efforts; of one-sided tolerance; of politically correct restraint on the battlefield; and of the inane effort to win "hearts and minds" rather than victories. When the goal of victory is achieved, there will be time to appeal to the hearts and minds of those left standing. Until then, it is quite simply "them" – or "us." We must choose to live or to die. Political correctness which disallows "profiling" or limits our ability to wage war with both maximum offense and defense is opening up the terrible possibilities for consequences even more chilling.

The recent nuclear test by N. Korea and the continued nuclear program of Iran are harbingers of what is to come from the East. It is just a matter of time before Muslim fanatics use nuclear weapons to attack the West. *It is simply a matter of time.* Those preaching restraint, patience, and U.N. style diplomacy rather than preemption will have to accept the consequences of their appeasement.

If the threat of terrorism outside our country is clear, it should be too with respect to domestic violence, but it's not. Our cities are overrun with violent gangs and we treat the condition with more social programs and midnight basketball. Our schools are turned into battlegrounds for deranged killers and we meekly ask the social "scientists" why? The reasons are clear – but political correctness inhibits our ability to implement solutions.

Certainly, there has always been violence, and there have always been madmen (and women!). In recent years, though, we have witnessed more and more senseless attacks on innocent people – often children. Is the media just portraying the awful events more, or are they really taking place more often? I believe the latter. The real question is, however, "what is the proper response?"

For twenty years or so, a culture of sleaze and violence has been tolerated in our society and thrived amid protections against "censorship" and "free markets." Do-gooders have defended the exposure of more and more graphic products with sexual and violent themes to impressionable young minds. The result is predictable to the most naïve analysis. It is not rocket science to see the preoccupation with sex and violence, the loss of regard for life and living things, and the irreverence for all that is good and wholesome resulting from the barrage of garbage thrown at young people.

It goes beyond the "copycat" crimes that inevitably follow each terrible act of violence - and there have been too many "Columbines." No, the damage is much deeper - perhaps endemic - in a generation electronically tethered to the most vile behavioral indoctrination of video games, music, and movies – and we have systematically allowed it to happen. The business and entertainment communities want profits and care not a whit about the destruction of generations of young minds and hearts. They should be taken to task; accomplices to violence cannot be tolerated. This is not censorship, it is a reinstatement of reasonable cultural values essential to the functioning of any civilization.

We have the means to deal with violence – around the world and at home. We simply have to use the proper response. Unfortunately, we cannot afford to exhibit the grace shown by the Amish in their personal tragedy. We are facing even larger evils that threaten our entire way of life; in our cities, around the country, and throughout our world. Nothing short of overwhelming force will protect us from the threats we face. We had better begin using it.

§

WHAT *IS* THE MAINSTREAM? (MAY 2003)

"A great deal has been said about my commitment not to raise taxes. It's a core value - it's common sense - it's important to keeping and growing jobs - and it's mainstream!"
        ~ Gov. Timothy Pawlenty

Politicians and pundits are fond of talking about the "mainstream," some imagined zone which reflects the middle of the bell-shaped curve of American thought, philosophy, and values. Although the term is cited to accept or reject federal judges, pillory politicians with differing views, or trash other journalists or analysts who operate in a different philosophical band, the "mainstream" is generally undefined; and conveniently so. In that manner it can be suggested that those of differing opinions are outside of it!

In reality, those on the left of American thought have high-jacked a convenient term for their benefit. The real mainstream, the center of American values and philosophies, has been marginalized; that is, pushed off to the side, and characterized as "the right." The Liberals have done so in an attempt to artificially move their left-leaning agendas closer to the center. Through political correctness and indoctrination, many have accepted this self-defined "center" as mainstream when nothing could be further from the truth. The education establishment, public employees, unions, special interest groups, much of our media, and most of our liberal politicians continue to push this non-mainstream agenda as if it reflected the values and positions of most Americans. It does not.

An issue by issue analysis is instructive to find out what the mainstream really is. We have selected a number of contemporary issues for illustration. These views are often characterized as right-leaning by the major media, though we would submit that they are closer to the *true* mainstream. We'll let the readers judge.

Abortion: The killing of an unborn child is generally held as morally wrong. There are issues such as rape, incest and others that complicate the legal position of society in the matter, just as killing any human being is complicated by issues of self-defense, a just war, and other circumstances. While society may tolerate abortion in limited circumstances, it is not an act simply to be exercised as a matter of choice. There have to be compelling reasons for its justification at the societal level, and even then subject to the personal moral values of the mother and father of the unborn child.

Capital Punishment and Criminals: As noted, the taking of a human life is generally wrong. The ultimate justice for the commission of a violent, premeditated and often heinous capital crime is death of the offender. It is also the only absolute deterrent against the offender commiting the crime again. Issues of age and mental capacity are justifiable factors to consider in some degree, but they do not fully mitigate the right of a civilized world to insure against such violent acts. Habitual criminals demonstrate contempt for reasonable rules of civilization and through their own actions limit their freedom and access to personal enjoyment proportionate to their offenses; and in the case of serious offenders, that should be precious little.

Economy/Employment: The government creates neither jobs nor wealth. Capitalism has been shown to best ensure broadbased individual freedom of choice and prosperity. All jobs are created, and the highest potential for wealth through achievement is offered, when individuals are minimally constrained to exercise their ingenuity and freedom of choice. Natural talents, hard work, and personal choices may reward or limit the ability of one to achieve material success, but that is a far better set of factors than those imposed by a government, a monarch, or a dictator.

Education: Our government is fond of reminding us that driving is a privilege, and passes any number of rules to regulate us. So too, public education is a privilege, and there are rules of behavior that are reasonably expected as a condition for participation. There have come to be a great many rights, however, but few duties or expectations.

Insubordination, even violence, is met with a slap on the wrist. There *is* a mission for public education, and that includes proficiency in the primary bodies of knowledge, the teaching of values that reflect good citizenship, and the acquisition of basic life skills. The education system has increasingly failed in this mission, encroached on family values, and substituted "feel good" results for solid academic performance.

Environment: All life is dependent upon the protection and preservation of the environment in which we live. We are bound by our own desire for self-preservation to be good stewards of the land, seas and other life with which we share our planet. That is no reason, however, to deny the use of natural resources for our benefit. The needs of human beings are not subservient to the preservation of an arbitrarily defined "species" of weed, worm, or moth. Sensitivity to the environment has to allow for the reasonable needs and desires of people and society.

Family: The family is the most fundamental unit of socialization and civilization. It is defined not only by our social structure, but by God and nature, as a husband/father, a wife/mother, children, and extended family comprised of other relatives and intimate friends. Society ought to do those things that protect, encourage, and nurture this fundamental building block, and discourage or prohibit those things that weaken, undermine, or contribute to its decline. The standard should not be lowered because of individual failings; and each of us who fail should acknowledge our shortcomings and try harder.

Federalism: A concern from the outset of America's founding, and an ever-growing factor in its recent history, the growth of the federal government has been accompanied by a diminution of the rights and powers of the states and of individual citizens. The safeguards against an all-powerful central government elite have been watered down beyond recognition and created immense concern. Federal funding is used more and more as an illegitimate enticement or coercive club to force behavior on states that should instead be reserved to them.

Foreign Policy: Our foreign policy should focus fundamentally on protection from our enemies, the encouragement of trade, and the facilitation of relationships which respect the mutual sovereignty of nations. There is no legitimate duty to fund other countries, or to aid or interfere with their operation except for our own benefit or that of our allies. To the extent that peace, trade, and friendship is fostered, benevolent financial and other policies are beneficial.

Government/Taxes: Thomas Paine summed it up succinctly: *"That government governs best that governs least."* Taxes are legitimate only to the extent they fund the reasonable, necessary, and constitutional needs of the government created by the people. They become excessive, burdensome, and even tyrannical when they exceed that end.

Gun Control: The 2nd amendment is clear from both its stated and its historically understood purpose. The government of a free people is restrained from natural excess only when the individual citizens are free to remain armed. Though armies be great, it is a citizenry armed to protect against despotism that is the great psychological equalizer against any government. The right to bear arms is not merely for hunting or home defense; it is to preserve freedom from tyranny.

Health Care: The health care system worked when it was largely comprised of doctors and other care providers; hospitals and care facilities; scientists and researchers; and patients. It started to break when it was consumed by government regulation, insurance companies, HMOs, and other creations of government and bureaucracy. Fifty years of intrusion by these institutions have made it worse, not better. More government involvement can only accelerate the decline, increase the costs, and diminish the service.

Homosexuality: It matters not whether genetic or by choice; the behavior is unnatural, contrary to the fundamental duty to encourage traditional families, and morally offensive to the large majority. As a private matter between consenting adults, society has no need or right to infringe upon it, just as it has no need or right to infringe upon other strictly personal behavioral choices. As a public matter, it has every need and right to do so, however; and this is the fundamental distinction.

Immigration: We are a nation of immigrants, and few would argue against the long tradition of welcoming those who work hard, contribute as productive citizens, and live according to the rules, traditions, and established language and culture of our nation. The violation of reasonable rules of entry, and the abuse of access to education, health care, and other benefits of society is not tolerable, nor should it be rewarded. It should be treated as the criminal behavior that it clearly is.

Judicial Activism: The historic distrust of the power of judges is well founded today as many appointed to this powerful post have abused it for personal and political agendas. The function of interpreting and enforcing the laws of the land has been perverted, with no better example than the recurring attacks on the Constitution by the 9th Circuit Court. This most overturned court in history is a prime example of the excess spawned by judicial activism, rather than responsibility and restraint.

Language and Culture: Ours is a western culture, based on a Judeo-Christian moral philosophy, Western European (especially English) culture, English language, and the legal traditions of a constitutional republic and English common law. It embodies tolerance of differences, but not at the expense of its fundamental character.

Media: A free press is constitutionally protected and historically rooted. Ever more concentrated corporate ownership of the press and all other media, political correctness, and other factors have subverted the basic purpose and made our media the subject of increasing mistrust or indifference.

Military/Veterans: Those serving in our military are among the most respected and revered in society because they put the cause of freedom above even their own lives. The overwhelming might of our armed forces is testament not simply to the advances of our technology, but to the power of freedom and personal conviction. Those who serve, and those who have served, are deserving of our utmost respect and appreciation as a free people.

Politicians/Term Limits: The notion of the citizen-politician has lost favor to a patrician elite in which those elected serve for life, and are followed by their family members to continue an unearned legacy. The power and privilege of those in politics has become so abused and self-serving that only objective term limits can pry them from office, and then only after they have bestowed upon themselves a lifetime of continued financial rewards and benefits.

Property Rights: The right to own and peacefully enjoy one's personal private property is among our most fundamental rights. There are reasonable restraints such as zoning laws, public ownership of mineral and water rights in developed areas, and similar limits. Increasingly, however, ownership rights are being diminished or taken entirely for much more flimsy reasons – and that is wrong.

Race: Discrimination on the basis of race, origin, or ethnicity is wrong. It is legally wrong, as it should be, in matters of public access or accommodation, and morally wrong even as a matter of private choice. The freedom of private choice is, however, a greater right and no government has a right to dictate to individuals how they should think or act within their personal sphere. Special preference or exclusion in the public arena is wrong no matter to whom it is applied. Racial preferences, quotas, and similar programs are wrong. Period.

Religion/Traditional Values: The philosophy enshrined in our Christian history is a cornerstone of our public position on religion. A belief in God is fundamental to our political system, as is tolerance of all beliefs, including the right of holding none; the adoption of a particular state sanctioned and supported church is not. It is a perversion of our culture, and an affront to our founding principles, however, to reject our Godly nature in order to affirm our public acceptance of religious choice.

Welfare / Poverty: Poverty is a condition of choice as much as of circumstance. In a free society, which provides public education, widespread information, and relatively open access to virtually all opportunities, there is little justification for long-term, structural poverty. As a compassionate and able people, we respond to genuine need with generosity. In times of personal or widespread calamity, the outpouring of aid is predictably strong. The failure of citizens to make right choices does not however, confer upon them entitlement status, to be paid for by society generally or by other citizens.

These are not the views of the Left or the so-called Progressives. They are not the views espoused in elite academic settings, or at Hollywood cocktail parties. These are certainly not the positions taken by network television or major newspapers. They *are* the perspective, however, of most Americans who continue to view the world from right of center. Americans who base their positions on reason, not just feelings; who are concerned with justice for all people, not just the few; and who, when all else fails them, rely on that good old standby: *common sense.* It serves them well.

§

ENTITLED (JUN 2009)

"The U.S. Constitution doesn't guarantee happiness, only the pursuit of it. You have to catch up with it yourself."
  ~ Benjamin Franklin

Life, liberty and the pursuit of happiness – that's basically it. Oh, there are other enumerated rights to be sure, but mostly to ensure these fundamental guarantees. Our Constitution makes no mention of rights to education, health care, a job, a home, a car, food or public assistance when the going gets tough. It presumes that the right to be free places those burdens upon us, individually. We have come a long way from that concept. We have become *entitled...* and in the process, no longer free.

Health Care
The current debate is allegedly about providing health care. In reality, health care is available to us all, including our personal duty to make healthy choices in our lifestyles - which we often don't. The fact is, the debate is not about the availability of health care, but instead, *nationalizing* health care and controlling the process by which it is administered and dispensed. It is more about power than health.

The health care system, like so many other societal institutions, began to falter when the government – mostly federal – assumed an unconstitutional authority to meddle, to control, to punish, and to reward. It did so like it always does – incrementally, with initial forays into helping the most visible "victims:" the poor, the aged, and the disabled. Then expanding its reach to women and the children. Now it seeks to complete its control with expansion to all. Universal coverage is the mantra; universal control is the reality.

The Congress cannot perform its primary function of assuring safety and freedom from invasion, yet it expands into areas for which is has no constitutional authority. We have been savagely attacked on our own soil; we are living with terrorists in our midst; and we have been invaded by 20 million who have brazenly penetrated our borders. Still, Congress feels it necessary to protect us from doctors and nurses. Congress can barely manage its own affairs, yet it seeks to fix the world's best medical system it insists is broken.

We, and we alone, are entitled to make life choices that affect our health. *We* are entitled to select medical professionals in whom we trust as to their competencies and judgment. *We* are entitled to organize and support medical facilities in our communities, and to patronize purveyors of medical, pharmaceutical, and other products which aid in good health. We are *not*, however, entitled to health care as a government guaranteed right.

Housing
In the early days of our country, we found shelter of our own making. Whether a temporary encampment, a short term stay at an inn or lodge, in the comfort of friends or relatives, or in acquiring or constructing a dwelling of our own, we addressed the basic need for refuge from the elements and for a place to call "home."

Depending on our birth circumstances and our willingness to work and succeed, our economic capacity would vary. Depending on our economic capacity, the type and level of our accommodations would vary. There was no guarantee of either economic success or housing; it was a matter of personal circumstances and choice. It was neither equal among people, nor guaranteed to them.

Until recent decades, the situation was the same. Some lived on estates, some lived in apartments, and some stayed with friends, relatives, or roommates, as either a temporary or permanent condition.

Now we have government guarantees of housing, government funding of housing, government loan guarantees, and every imaginable involvement of government in the housing realm.

The current U.S. Department of Housing and Urban Development includes $38.5 billion for:
• Minority home ownership
• State and local block grants for affordable housing
• Self-help grants (sweat equity)
• Housing vouchers
• Housing counseling
• University partnership grants, including historically black colleges and Hispanic-serving institutions
• Affordable rental assistance (focus on Native Americans)
• Homeless assistance ($10 billion since 2001)
• Katrina victims
• Disabled and elderly
• HIV/AIDS housing
• Veterans
• Lead based paint remediation
• Community development
• Equal opportunity
• Faith-based and community initiatives (such as ACORN)

The federal government has no business doing virtually *any* of this. To the extent that citizens want to provide humanitarian assistance, it can and should be done at the state or local level, through private charitable institutions, or direct voluntary aid. We are *not* entitled to housing as a government guaranteed right.

Education
Historically, public education has been part of American culture, at least at the basic level and under the control of local or state governments. It was not an entitlement so much as a recognition of the societal benefits of knowledge, language, and enlightenment. Another purpose of public education was freedom from religious bias in church run schools. Of course, we have simply substituted government indoctrination for religious bias in our current model.

Education early on favored the white and the wealthy, make no mistake about it. That did not stop Benjamin Franklin, whose family could not afford to send him to college, from becoming the pre-eminent American scientist of his time and a key element in the founding of the nation. Neither did it prevent the poorly educated Thomas Paine from fueling a revoluiton with the passionate words of his reasoned essays.

Over the years, the American educational system became the envy of the world, and public secondary schools such as the University of California competed for the best minds along with the more esteemed private institutions. All of this with little support, or interference, from the federal government.

Today, unions and federal intervention have diminished the public education system in quality, functionality, and innovation. Schools have become agents of the bureaucracy, bloated and financially demanding far beyond justifiable need, draining the public treasury and producing citizens ill-equipped for the support of their country or even themselves. Graduates of primary schools do not possess the literacy or math and science ability needed to compete at the highest levels. Colleges have become parking places for incubating adolescents for 6-8 years or longer while students decide "what they want to be." The entire system has become nationalized – *and broken.*

Locally run, responsible, and productive educational systems are a benefit to society and its citizens and should be supported. Education is a pathway to our pursuit of happiness, but education from kindergarten through graduate school is not a government guaranteed right.

Employment

Like many Americans of my time, I started out my employment as a paperboy. (Today, I would be referred to as a "Publication Distribution Agent.") I have worked ever since. I worked throughout high school and college, part-time during the school year and full-time during the summers. I somehow managed to participate in sports and other activities in high school and still graduate. I never received a government grant, government training, or any government assistance in getting a job – yet I always had one. I never worked for the government, save the three years I gave to my country as a volunteer in the U.S. Army and part-time public teaching positions. My experience is not uncommon.

Somehow, we have arrived at a point where the government is the primary employment trainer, re-trainer, safety net, and employer of first resort. Government claims to "create jobs" as one of its primary duties. When employment falls, as it drastically has in the present economy, government claims to have limited the decline and to be capable of even reversing it.

The reality is simple: government creates no jobs except for those needed to administer its own, non-wealth creating bureaucracy and a handful of essential public services. Jobs are created when private capital, risk, management, labor, and materials come together to produce goods and services meeting the desires of free markets. Jobs are something we seek in response to our need to provide for ourselves and to pursue our own happiness. We are *not* entitled to a job as a government guaranteed right.

Transportation

I bought my first car for $350 when I was sixteen – a 1931 Model-A Ford. I had worked for the money to buy the car, and as my parents required, had the money for insurance and operating costs by way of my non-government provided part-time jobs. Prior to that, I had a bicycle, the ability to walk, and local public transportation: *the bus*. There was little or no federal transit, nor any federal transit money. There was an interstate highway system – the later creation of which was probably one of the early mistakes in letting the federal government exceed its legitimate scope!

Over the years, the regulatory and financing power of the federal government has grown to the point where there are few private transportation choices or responsibilities. Billions of dollars are thrown at "mass transit" projects though only 2% of the country uses them. Planes, trains, and automobiles are subject to extreme levels of regulation and now, choices are being forced on citizens to comply with the global warming police. Some actually want GPS devices installed on cars so government can track your whereabouts (in the name of fuel efficiency, of course).

Car companies are failing, airline companies are losing their shirts, and trains – always insolvent – don't run on time, or collide with each other. Automobiles run over roads that are congested, over bridges that are unsound, and on gas from oil supplied by our enemies. The whole institution of transportation is a regulatory mess. The common denominator: *federal government*. Yes, there is a role for government in transportation, including public transit, but it is mostly state and local. The role of government is to provide the public infrastructure to accommodate our private choices. We are *not*, however, entitled to transportation as a government guaranteed right.

Public Assistance
My paternal grandmother would often boast proudly of her 16 children, always with the addendum that they were all by one man - and none of them on welfare. My grandparents were immigrants (legal) and farmers. Hard work and large families were a way of life. *Welfare was not.*

Seventy years later, welfare in one form or another has become a way of life for many. There are food stamps, housing assistance, job placement, education, health care, child care. and many more expectations and entitlements. There are direct payments to elevate one's income, even grants for digital television converters or gas-hog car trade-ins. It is a never-ending cornucopia of goodies provided by the federal government and paid for by the American citizens, against their will and without their consent. These entitlements are simply taken from one person and given to another.

Americans are kind and generous people. The vast majority would support reasonable services to provide for those truly unable to provide for themselves. They would give personally, and through their church or other charitable group for the same needs. Compassion for others is personal, voluntary, and a moral good. When such kindness is usurped by government, however, and institutionalized as "entitlements," it is simply one more form of tyranny. When the usurpation is at the federal level, the felony is compounded by the bureaucracy created and the distance from the user, encouraging abuse and fraud.

The worst part is, it's not even about the entitlements anymore; it's about the votes that granting and expanding entitlements buy for politicians. It's about the self-interest and perpetuation in office of our "leadership." And that, fellow Americans, is where the problem lies. The solution should be obvious.

"A government that is big enough to give you all you want is big enough to take it all away."
    ~ Barry Goldwater

§

CHAPTER 6

IMMIGRATION

In his 2007 State of the Union speech, Mexico's President Calderon railed against recent U.S. deportations of illegal aliens, denouncing these actions as "persecution" of "undocumented Mexican workers." Calderon declared: "Mexico does not end at the border, ... wherever there is a Mexican, Mexico is there."

JOBS AMERICANS WON'T DO? (AUG 2007)

Fifty years ago, I got my first job as a newspaper carrier for the Santa Clara Journal. I was ten years old. More importantly, I was proud. Work has that effect on young people. I had responsibilities, trust and ultimately, the confidence that comes with succeeding at any positive task. My experience was far from unusual. It was the norm to grow up working, and to continue to do so as a life long endeavor in one field or another. That's what people did – and they typically started early.

The work ethic isn't entirely gone, but it's endangered. Kids today seem to think that a personal television set, computer, cell phone, iPod, CD/ Stereo and high priced video game set are automatic. You simply ask – and things show up. Working for them is a bit novel. In the worst case, you wait for birthday or Christmas money from the relatives to get your entitlements. Once they turn 16, the mind-set of today's non-working kids reaches its zenith, with the expectation of a car, usually new and expensive – *and unearned.*

The popular apology for illegal immigrants is that they are doing the jobs Americans won't do. I question this. Yes, they are doing jobs many Americans are not doing, but "not doing" is very different from "won't do." Before waves of illegal immigration over the past 25 years, all the jobs that Americans "won't do" somehow got done – by Americans. What changed?

Jobs ARE done
Maids and other service staff of major hotels in populated areas are often illegal immigrants. So are construction, landscape, fast food, and agricultural workers. But this ignores the reality that in many parts of the country, these jobs get done by American workers. There are Americans doing dangerous work in coal mines, washing windows on high-rise buildings, and most any other job one considers. Where Illegals are, they take jobs; where they aren't, able-bodied Americans get the jobs done. The substitution of illegal workers is as much a simple matter of location as anything else.

Government's Role
By pushing minimum wage laws that have nothing to do with the cost-value relationship of labor, government artificially inflates the cost of low-end entry-level jobs. These are typically jobs requiring little education, no skills or training, and involving minimal risk. If they involved any of these things, they wouldn't be low-paying jobs! Bleeding heart liberals trot out stories of executive compensation excesses and talk about supporting a family on minimum wage to advance a socialist agenda. The reality is that these jobs are entry level; they are not intended to support families; they are intended to meet basic needs in society and encourage the individuals to advance through hard work, holding down multiple jobs, and getting an education or training. These jobs are a means, not an end. School age kids, recent legal immigrants, housewives, and other part-time workers used to fill these jobs.

Government can play a positive role, but it fails to do so. There are millions of people receiving "free" money ranging from education grant recipients to welfare dependents. These are Americans typically at the low end of the labor pool. Put them to work – doing the jobs Americans won't do. State and local governments can carry out such programs without the necessity of another federal bureaucracy – so long as the courts and the ACLU are kept at bay.

Work Stigma

There is no honest labor that is unworthy of respect. Why then are entry-level and unskilled jobs maligned by the media, academia, and pop-culture? The reality is that anyone providing a product or service is enhancing the lives of others. There is nothing wrong with starting at the bottom – but we make it seem so. Even skilled trades and services are treated as if they are less worthy than someone in the mindless bureaucracy where nothing is produced and no real service is provided.

Role of immigrants

In the illegal immigration debate, it has become commonplace to cite how "immigrants built this country." The omitted word – *illegal* – tells the real story. Throughout our history, and especially in the late 19th and early 20th centuries, immigrants coming largely from Europe filled most of the entry-level jobs which were needed, but required little in the way of special accomodation. My maternal grandmother, a legal Portuguese immigrant worked in the factories of New Bedford when she first arrived on our shore. She worked hard, never took a dime of welfare, never committed a crime, and went on to open her own successful restaurant while in her 60s! She spoke broken English but worked hard – proudly. She was typical of the immigrant population in those times.

The problem we face today is not too many immigrants, but too few – legal immigrants, that is. We have increased the number of immigrants and "temporary" workers at the upper end, but not at the entry level. Those illegally arriving in the entry-level category are less well educated, speak little English, and often include criminal and other undesirable elements. They often bring cultural backgrounds and propensities in conflict with our own. The diversity nuts love having America filled with the most needy and ill-trained dregs of the 3rd world. While the glut of Illegals bringing little continues to overload the country, many from western oriented countries, and with higher skills and dedication to American principles, are denied legal entry. The Kennedy immigration policies of the 1960s are a failure and we need to reinvent a working system of legal immigration – and a pool of responsible Americans to fill entry-level jobs.

To the extent that a need for seasonal employment exists (largely in agriculture), we need to reinvent a system that provides opportunities for legal, temporary adult workers. They come here as healthy, single adults for needed periods and then go home. They are not put on a path to citizenship simply because we have given them a job. They do not bring their families with them – if they desire to, they apply for legal permanent entry. If they become pregnant or ill, they are sent home. If they come here illegally, they are barred from eligibility in legal temporary worker programs and punished. They neither pay into, nor are eligible for, social security. They pay a flat tax deducted by their employers, who also provide health, housing, transportation and basic needs while employed. Why is this so hard to understand?

Spoiled, Lazy Kids

America's youth used to fill a large number of entry-level jobs. As a kid, I worked as a dishwasher, busboy, construction laborer, and other menial positions for which I was decently paid, and rewarded with a sense of performing honest work. I even cut "cots" (apricots cut for drying), a rite of passage growing up in the agriculturally rich Santa Clara Valley. Kids today are protected from the horror of *hard work*. Parents seem more obsessed with their kids having the latest in tech toys, while bothering little to encourage or instill a work ethic. Much is given; little is expected in return. Many of these kids could and should be doing the jobs "that Americans won't do." They just need a gentle but guiding kick in the butt to get out and do them.

For the few kids who do seek out entry-level jobs, they are greeted with a non-English speaking environment which is threatening if not downright hostile. I watched recently as a young man thumbed through a rack of employment applications at a local fast food restaurant. "Do you have one of these in English?" the boy asked. Sure enough, the entire stack was in Spanish. We have created a climate in some entry-level jobs where speaking English and being an American is an intrusion into a foreign work culture which dominates such fields of employment.

Education is oversold

We have become a nation of both under and over-educated idiots. The education establishment doesn't care. Their sole motivation is to keep the floodgates open for all to enter their lofty institutions – and get more public money to "educate" them all.

It is a heresy to suggest that not everyone is qualified to go to college. The University of Nevada recently implemented a small increase in required grades for admission. When it became apparent that minority acceptances were down, the university did what universities do in such situations. They re-lowered the standards. After all, diversity and universal education are more important than qualifications. In reality, we are "educating" far too many, especially in marginally employable subject areas. We have multitudes of educated idiots with degrees in esoteric subjects, but a shortage of plumbers, electricians and brick layers. The education establishment disparages manual labor, blue-collar work, and sales, while promoting college courses of questionable worth. If we steered more young Americans into trades for which they are more qualified and would likely have more interest, we'd have fewer Illegals taking those well paying jobs. In addition, we might actually see a cut in spending for education which has been oversold.

If education fails at the low end, it does at the upper end as well. We neither motivate nor educate very well in primary grades for mathematics, science, and engineering fields. Parents are greatly at fault as well. American kids are told to follow their dreams and aspirations; Asian kids are told to study mathematics and science. Those fields are just too objective and demanding for spoiled American kids. There's no room for "feelings" in answers, only facts. That doesn't square with the warm and fuzzy world that many parents want their little darlings to live in.

While the problem of over-educating invites illegal immigrants to fill the void in trades and manual labor, the problem of under-educating erodes the participation of Americans in favor of temporary skilled workers and immigrants without the same cultural heritage. This undue reliance on non-citizens and recent immigrants is unhealthy. Ask England, whose very culture is under assault by Muslim "workers" who are taking over the country.

There are few jobs Americans won't do; there are many that they either can't do, or are discouraged from doing. Parents, educators, and policy makers need to start addressing the issue or it will be too late. We allow too many well paying jobs to go to those here illegally – that has to stop. We don't provide a system for qualified and hard-working immigrants from western nations to come here to work legally and become productive citizens – that has to change. We don't instill a work ethic in our kids; instead we encourage a sense of entitlement, instant gratification, and laziness – that is destructive to our values and culture. We send idiots to college to appease the academic elite, while discouraging honest work in meaningful and necessary trades – that is just plain stupid. We honor philosophically the concept of labor, but denigrate and demean real work.

Let's return to the common sense reality that there are NO jobs that Americans won't do, given the proper education, experience, motivation, and opportunity.

"Opportunity is missed by most people because it is dressed in overalls and looks like work."
    ~ Thomas A. Edison

§

FRAMING THE IMMIGRATION DEBATE (NOV 2007)

"In the first place, we should insist that if the immigrant who comes here in good faith becomes an American and assimilates himself to us, he shall be treated on an exact equality with everyone else, for it is an outrage to discriminate against any such man because of creed, or birthplace, or origin. But this is predicated upon the person's becoming in every facet an American and nothing but an American... There can be no divided allegiance here. Any man who says he is an American, but something else also, isn't an American at all. We have room for but one flag, the American flag... We have room for but one language here, and that is the English language... and we have room for but one sole loyalty and that is a loyalty to the American people."
    ~ *Theodore Roosevelt*

The United States is now home to an estimated 20 million people who have entered this country illegally, largely from Mexico and Central America. The political and social debates have assuredly failed to address the real issues surrounding this problem. Appeals to emotion have been used to support political motivations, while rational discussions have been slammed as inhumane; both at great risk to the country.

The Popular Discussion
The apologists for illegal immigration don't really see it as a problem. Or, worse, they know it is a problem, but continue to ignore the substantial negative aspects for political reasons. What we hear are trite, emotion-driven apologies and irrational or unsupportable explanations:

- They are pursuing economic opportunity and the "American Dream."
- It punishes the children.
- It's the only country they know.
- Deportation is damaging as it separates families.
- Illegal immigrants live in an atmosphere of terror and mistrust.
- They are doing the jobs Americans won't do.

- This nation was built by immigrants.
- There are too many to deport; it's impractical.
- We need comprehensive immigration reform.
- Get them out of the shadows and on a pathway to citizenship.
- They are victims of traffickers and greedy employers.
- We need employer verification and punishment for offenders.
- They must pay a fine and learn English.
- Build a fence and secure the borders.
- If we don't educate them, they will just joing gangs.
- If we don't provide medical services, they will infect others.

The Real Issues

Invasion

Hundreds of foreign citizens have illegally entered the country each year for decades. They came here for political refuge, to escape family or other life traumas, or to seek a better life. Their numbers were small, their hearts were pure, and their motives were true. They spoke or quickly learned English on their own, expecting no special accommodation. They worked hard at less desirable jobs without public assistance or special programs. They assimilated American culture and principles; they left the flag and philosophy of their home country behind. Americans looked the other way as to their immigration status. We preferred they come legally, but these were decent, hard-working people who wanted to embrace Lady Liberty. We took them in, looked after them and encouraged them to succeed – and they did.

That has changed. We now have 12-20 million or more Illegal aliens having invaded the country in uncontrollable hordes. They come here to work, but also to traffic in drugs and other crime. Their allegiance is to their home country and culture, though they freely take the benefits of this one in well-paying jobs; add to that free education, health services, and the prospect of easy citizenship by giving birth to an "anchor" baby – at the public's expense. They expect accommodation in language, culture and and other special wants to boot. *The "immigrant" comparison is hardly the same.*

Security

While many arriving here come for and find work, many others are here for criminal and even terrorist purposes. The ease with which our southern border can be penetrated offers a welcome mat to vicious gangs as well as Muslim terrorists. The northern border, while less active, is equally easy to traverse. We are doing little to prevent this and likely have thousands if not hundreds of thousands of people waiting to unleash harm and terror on Americans; many of them now American citizens.

According to a 2006 report of the House Committee on Homeland Security's Subcommittee on Investigations, the Border Patrol apprehended 1.2 million illegal aliens attempting to enter the United States in 2005. The report mentioned that those caught were a fraction of the estimated 4 to 10 million illegal aliens who tried to enter the United States that year. Ominously, the report also states: *"Members of Hezbollah have already entered the United States across the Southwest border."*

Crime

According to the U.S. Border Patrol, the numerous major crimes appear on the records of previously deported illegal aliens including: Kidnapping, Homicide, and Sexual assault. Dangerous drugs comprise a very large percentage of crimes. Not a day goes by in which there is not a report of a crime committed by an illegal alien who apologists say, "simply wanted to pursue the American dream!" Of course, existing citizens commit such crimes as well, but a high proportion of crime and gang activity is related to illegal immigrants. The Washington Times reports that illegal aliens comprise between 6 percent and 10 percent of Virginia's jail population and about 2 percent of the state's prison population. According to the Federation for American Immigration Reform, in 1980, federal and state prisons housed fewer than 9,000 criminal aliens. By the end of 1999, the same prisons housed over 68,000 criminal aliens. Criminal aliens presently account for over 29 percent of prisoners in Federal Bureau of Prisons facilities. *This country has plenty of crime – we don't need to import more.*

Identity theft

In addition to violent crime, there is rampant theft of citizen's identifications. Adding to the problem is the criminal behavior of cities like New York which knowingly issue driver's licenses to illegal aliens, paving the way for still further misuse of identification documents.

Health

Recently, a Mexican national was found to carry a highly infectious form of tuberculosis. This individual had illegally entered the country by various modes 76 times. In 2001, tuberculosis cases were studied by the Indiana School of Medicine and found to have originated from illegal Mexican immigrants. Other infectious diseases including cholera, plague, leprosy, smallpox, and others are showing up with increasing frequency along our borders and border towns, only to be spread further as illegal migrants move freely throughout the country. What will be the cost of an epidemic breakout of any of these diseases? What will be the loss of life?

Economic costs

The direct costs of illegal immigration are highly visible: Education systems with runaway budgets trying to accommodate both the language deficiencies and sheer number of illegal students attending school with our federal government's express consent. The cost of both crime, and the associated costs of incarcerating criminals, is properly the expense of the native country of the perpetrators, but Americans are bearing the burden. Hospital emergency rooms are treated as outpatient clinics by illegal residents, while pre-natal, delivery and post-natal services for their babies are provided free of charge. Americans pay the cost in higher taxes and insurance premiums. *The federal government says they must!*

Harvard economics professor George Borjas, has determined that the base cost of illegal aliens to the nation's economy is around $70 billion annually, in addition to more than $133 billion in job-loss costs to American workers. A 2007 study written by Dr. Robert Rector of the Heritage Foundation, calculates that the potential price tag to taxpayers for granting amnesty to the millions of illegal aliens now here could top $2.5 trillion! The entire current federal budget is roughly $3 trillion. Thank you Senators Kennedy, McCain and Reid - as well as President Bush and other "moderate" Republicans.

Economic loss

Remittances by Mexican workers in the U.S. to Mexico constitute the 2nd largest economic sector for that country, exceeded only by energy and followed by tourism. This is a great boon for Mexico and a huge loss to the U.S. economy. Recent estimates put the number at $20 billion annually but it is likely much higher with cash carried as freely across the borders as immigrants themselves. With a reasonable multiplier effect, the drain on the U.S economy is probably $100 billion or more each year. No wonder Mexico resists changing the situation.

Dislocation of employment

We hear of the need for illegal migrants to fill jobs that Americans won't do. Whole industries have capitulated to this source of illegal and cheap labor, including: hotels and hospitality, casinos, construction and landscape, agriculture, and food processing. Is it truly the case that there are no American workers for these jobs? Or do such daunting majorities of non-English speaking Illegals intimidate Americans to simply forefeit opportunities? We have shifted our whole employment paradigm, not to benefit from illegal foreign labor but to be limited by it.

Dilution of culture

Seldom a day goes by when the news media is not trumpeting an event foreign to American culture and tradition, but extolling the way of life of Mexicans, Muslims, or other foreign experiences. Foreign street signs and language abound in many neighborhoods. We are expected to accommodate the needs of other languages and cultures far beyond what we'd expect in other countries. The issue has gone beyond a polite nod to the multi-cultural experience, or reasonable assistance to foreign visitors. It is instead pervasive and destructive to all that is historically American. The social fabric woven of western European traditions, Christian philosophy, and English language has been a unifying force since our nation's founding; it is being torn to shreds.

Rights and duties of sovereign states

This nation is a sovereign state and has a duty to protect its citizens from invasion – *it is not doing so*. Mexico, and other countries, have a duty to be responsible for the actions of their citizens, including the illegal trespass into this country – *they are not doing so*. Why are we not negotiating treaties to enforce these responsibilities? No, instead we are marching toward a North American Union which will virtually wipe out any semblance of sovereignty between the borders of Mexico and Canada. Our country is being taken from us right in front of our eyes, and facilitiated by our government. *Does that make you sleep well?*

Government created problems

These are the issues that need to frame the debate on illegal immigration. The Congress led by Harry Reid, however, is still trying to ram through some version of the Kennedy-McCain-Bush amnesty bill. They must be stopped. The recent attempts by Reid and others to pass the DREAM Act was just an incremental version of the same, targeting students and young people with free education and citizenship; parents and family to follow.

The Security and Prosperity Partnership (SPP) is nothing less than a means of wiping out the borders and sovereign rights of this nation; it is part, in fact, of an on-going movement promoting a dissolution of the United States as we know it and the creation of a superior world government. Don't believe me? Professor Robert Pastor, had this to say to the Senate Foreign Relations Committee in 2005, *"The best way to secure the United States is not at our borders with Mexico and Canada but at the borders of North America as a whole."* This goal, he said, *"we hope to accomplish by 2010."* Welcome to the New World Order.

While the feds are leading the charge, many states are not far behind, with "sanctuary cities" providing immunity with impunity from our immigration laws. New York is working on a Domestic Workers Bill of Rights to ensure rights to Illegals that many citizens don't even have. There are on-going efforts to make Social Security and Medicare, the SCHIP health insurance program, employment and additional education benefits available to illegal aliens – while many veterans have been cut off from medical or other VA programs!

Efforts to enforce the 14th amendment of the Constitution (*which does NOT confer citizenship on babies born to illegal residents*) continues to be thwarted by Harry Reid, Nancy Pelosi and the Congress they lead. Why? Because those so granted citizenship are likely future Democrats. For the same reason, we continue to favor immigration – legal and illegal – by uneducated, poor, non-English speaking 3rd world residents, with expansion of that base by a "chain migration" policy which brings the rest of their families. In such a manner, 20 million Illegals will become 100 million citizens – *all voting Democrat!*

These folks are not "undocumented workers," they are not simply "doing the work Americans won't do," and they are not simply one more wave of immigrants that make this country great while pursuing "the American dream." They represent a massive invasion and a costly and destructive element impacting economics, crime, education, health care, and culture. The current debate on illegal immigration is a charade and the real issues need to be put on the table. Until now, our political leaders have failed to do so. They have concealed, conspired, and lied. The truth needs an awakening.

"To build on the advances of the past decade and to craft an agenda for the future, we propose the creation by 2010 of a community to enhance security, prosperity, and opportunity for all North Americans. To that end, we propose a community based on the premise that each member benefits from its neighbor's success and is diminished by its problems. The boundaries of the community would be defined by a common external tariff and an outer security perimeter. Within this area, the movement of people and products would be legal, orderly, and safe. The overarching goal is to guarantee a free, safe, just, and prosperous North America."
      ~ Council on Foreign Relations

§

CHAPTER 7

WAR

"I venture to say no war can be long carried on against the will of the people."
    ~ Edmund Burke

THE IRAQ WAR - INEFFECTIVELY WAGED (MAY 2007)

The patience of Americans of all stripes is wearing thin. It is not because they don't have the stomach for war; it is not because they don't recognize and honor the sacrifice of our fighting men and women; and it is not because they support the pious pontifications of Democrats who want to bail for political advantage. No, Americans are tired of this war because it has been ineffectively waged from the outset. They have been tolerant because they love their country, they respect the office of the Presidency, and they respect the dedication of American fighting forces to protect and defend liberty.

There is a growing disconnect, however, between what we are doing and why. There is a growing realization that we are concerned about protecting the borders of Iraq, but not our own. There is a growing awareness that we are building hospitals in Iraq while Walter Reed is crumbling; that we are building schools for Iraqis while overcrowding our own; and that we are busy securing democracy in the middle east while ours is under attack.

Americans want to know why we are fighting among terrorists to protect Iraq rather than against terrorists in defense of our citizens at home. They want to know why it takes years to train Iraqi soldiers to defend themselves, while we send American troops to do their job with 6 months of training at home. They want to know why we are at war with Iraq as a sponsor of terrorism, and yet bringing 7,000 of them to live among us, and allowing hundreds of thousands of Muslims attend American universities.

The Basics

One problem with this war is that it involves neither identifiable enemies nor a single state sponsor. We are told that many Muslims are peaceful, yet radical Islam is at the center of most international violence. We are loath to connect any state to the "war" on terror, yet the entire Middle East and many in Islamic nations around the world are clearly connected. We are dependent on their oil and refuse to seek energy independence. Instead we play games. It's like tolerating rats simply because they keep the garbage down.

In fact, fighting this war is like exterminating rats. The enemy is much the same; worthless vermin that come out from walls and from under rocks and prey on innocents. Their numbers are large, their associations are loose, and their methods are insidious. Victory is not achieved by the signing of a treaty of surrender. The military objective in this war is not all-out victory, but rather containment and reduction of the enemy's capabilities; forcing it to live in the shadows… like rats.

A simple Formula for War

1. Sufficient Reason. War is ugly. There must be a sufficient, immediate and direct threat to the United States, its citizens, or its allies to justify war. Such a threat need not be sold to the American people - they will understand it, if it is explained. If the reason is not self-evident, it is not sufficient. The reason for this war has been neither self-evident nor has it been sufficient.

2. Formal Declaration. Only the Members of Congress can declare war according to our Constitution. They have not done so. Instead, to preserve their political options, they have authorized the president to take military action. In doing so, they have communicated a lack of commitment to our enemies and less than total support for our country. They have retained the options to criticize the Commander in Chief, to withhold financial support, to demand timetables, and to even visit with the enemy's leadership and conduct treasonous "diplomacy." This is congressional convenience; it is not war.

184 _____ Reason, Justice and Common Sense

3. Clearly Defined Objectives. Was the objective of this "war" to topple Saddam Hussein? Was it to protect and secure the oil fields of Iraq? Was it to establish a freely elected government? If it was any of these things, we could have achieved the objective and withdrawn. The fact is, we have never had clearly defined objectives - and we must, if we are to wage war effectively.

4. Use of Overwhelming Force. Once our objectives are defined, it is the job of our military to achieve them, without interference from politicians, without limitations in the use of force, while using the full might available to them, and unconstrained by political correctness. We cannot turn soldiers loose to kill an enemy and then put them on trial when they succeed. We cannot maintain the world's most powerful military arsenal and then fail to use it for swift and sure military victory. We are instead using American troops for target practice by every two-bit terrorist wannabe armed with an IED or suicide bomb. Our job must be to kill and destroy the capacity to kill and destroy us. There is no place for restraint. There can be no exclusion of religious halls as military targets. There can be no caving to international critics who have no dog in the fight but who will be the first to ask for our help when they are attacked.

5. Conclusion of Operations. When we are done, we are done. It is not our job to rebuild a nation vanquished as a result of its own stupid aggressions. If their people are decimated, and their landscape littered with debris, they can thank a faulty leadership in whom they wrongly placed their faith. They can also spend the coming decades rebuilding rather than destroying, and learn to take their place among a more civilized humanity. There can be no Marshall Plan when there is no unconditional surrender. When there is only a temporary withdrawal of rats, one does not rebuild their habitat.

This is a formula for war in this age. It has not been followed since WW II. If it had, the stories in Korea, Viet Nam and Iraq would be very different. If we do not come to accept these realities, the writing of our own future history may be very different too – and written by someone other than us.

Political Correctness and International law
The Geneva Conventions were written for conventional wars undertaken by identifiable nation states. They have no place in the world of terrorism and should be rejected and rewritten, unilaterally if necessary. When an enemy uses holy places to hide weapons; uses a 12 year-old to behead a civilian; uses human shields and suicide bombs, there is no set of rules for humanity. The provisions for duties of an occupying force, treatment of the enemy, and limitations on force go out the window. It is time to rewrite these outdated and self-defeating rules of warfare.

Pure Politics
While Ameicans do not like this war, they like the use of it for political purposes even less. When Harry Reid casually testifies to the war being lost, when Nancy Pelosi arrogantly meets with enemy states, and when a Democratic Congress thumbs its nose at the needs of the American military, Americans get angry. And then they get even.

It is no accident that our tendency to engage in war mirrors the decline in military service among the members of Congress and their families. While members of Congress are increasingly well-educated, they are also increasingly unwilling to serve. Only 27% of all Representatives and 35% of Senators have served in the Armed Forces. Fewer still have served in combat. About 1% of the children of members of Congress currently serve. For those who insist on racial stereotypes, 71% of those in the military serving in the Middle East Theater are white, and they account for 76% of the losses. Reinstatement of a "draft" may be necessary if for no other reason than to equalize the risk-taking by *all* Americans in the nation's defense.

Cost
This war has cost a half-trillion dollars already and may cost a trillion or more before any sort of conclusion. Americans are asking, "for what?" What if we had kept our military at home, protecting our nation and its borders? What if we had spent a trillion dollars on repositioning bases and troops along our borders? What if we invested in missile and other

defense systems? What if we invested in removing our dependency on oil from terrorist states? What if we just returned the money to the people to whom it belongs! There are a lot of questions – and few answers to justify the expenditure.

Cultural impact

After Viet Nam, we were flooded with Vietnamese war refugees. The 135,000 who initially came were joined by thousands of "boat people," followed by another 200,000 Amerasians and political prisoners. Today, Vietnamese and other Southeast Asians number over 1.8 million. President Bush has already authorized the resettlement of 7,000 Iraqis to this country. The culture of America is under dilution by 12-20 million illegal aliens and is likely to be subjected to hundreds of thousands more as liberal guilt takes hold. This time, the many who come are likely to have terrorists among them; and those terrorists are quite likely to possess nuclear weapons. Does this make sense to anyone?

The Alternative

If we are to be safe, secure within our borders, and respected around the world by our enemies and friends alike, we need to change the way we do things. Completely. Now.

We have become a laughing stock because we fail to use the power we possess. We invite illegal entry because we neither protect our borders, nor prosecute those who violate them. We are neither feared nor respected because we invent silly, politically correct rules to fight wars while enemies will stop at nothing to defeat us. It is our choice to restore sanity to our defense, or to lay fallen on the world's battlefields, consumed by rats. We'd better make our minds up soon.

"No bastard ever won a war by dying for his country. He won it by making the other poor dumb bastard die for his country."
  - George S. Patton

§

ANSWERING WAR CRITICS (FEB 2003)

"Let every nation know, whether it wishes us well or ill, that we shall pay any price, bear any burden, meet any hardship, support any friend, oppose any foe to assure the survival and the success of liberty."
      ~ John F. Kennedy

War is a terrible solution to conflict. It is a tragic loss of life and waste of resources that could be put to advancing the condition of mankind. Unfortunately, it is also a necessary response to the presence of evil. Just as revolution has been a radical but necessary response to despots governing nations, war has proven a necessary answer to those who would challenge and destroy other nations, or even risk world-wide holocaust for their selfish wickedness.

Unlike diplomacy, war is not a battle of words; and the results are not the loss of face. Diplomacy is the first effort to reconcile; war is the last response. To understand the necessity of war in the current situation, it is helpful to understand why critics are opposed.

Preemption
As a fair and moral nation, we have always been guided by a view of military action in response to provocation. In recent years, we have often been slow to respond to nominal attacks, even at the loss of American citizens and soldiers. When attacks were at the behest of nations and waged with conventional weaponry, such a delayed response was a civil posture. In a world of multi-national, or even rogue terrorists, with a potential for catastrophic loss from weapons of mass destruction, the rules have changed. Failing to act on reasonable intelligence indicating a potential for such modern acts of violence is stupid, and a constitutional breach of duty. The president had been right to move slowly and to use every tool to disarm our enemies peacefully. In the light of failure of those efforts, he has also been right to mass our military might for an overwhelming assault. The rapid decimation of the enemy should be his objective; the minimization of civilian casualties will, of course, be a

major goal; but the prevention of the loss of American lives will be his primary duty, and that may well justify preemptive action.

Unilateral Action

America is not a bully. We do not go around picking fights with lesser nations. Though our might stands alone, and our economic resources are many, our national character is of a warm and generous spirit. We are quick to offer assistance, and slow to anger. We have given back to nations that which might well be claimed as ours from the use of our technology, know-how, or other resources - *hardly an imperialist orientation.* We have not needed the permission of France, Germany, or the U.N. to act in our generosity, and we do not need it to act in our defense. We are a sovereign nation and, as such, have the right to act in any manner to protect our self-interest. That we welcome the support of just and freedom seeking allies is a reflection of our cooperative spirit, not a required mandate to act. When tyrants offend the sensibilities of the free world, it is desired that the free world will respond in unison. The failure of any of them, or all of them, to do so is a blight on their own national character, not a restraint on our own.

More Inspections

For 12 years, Iraq has been in default of directives from a patient world that allowed it to cleanse itself of past transgressions. It chose to ignore those generous offers and direct its limited wealth to hateful instead of peaceful devices. It built chemical and biological weapons, instead of an economy that would sustain its citizens. It ventured further into the realm of nuclear weapons for massive destruction of life and the advance of an evil agenda of one man. The sole purpose of any inspections were to allow this man one last chance to correct past wrongs, not to establish new ones. He failed to do so, and has placed his nation at risk. He is not entitled to one additional day of delay, nor one additional "inspection." He needs to go – and will. *It was his choice.*

Financial Costs

There is no financial measure, nor any financial constraint, to the preservation of freedom. Had there been, our own American revolution would have never been fought, and certainly would not have continued to secure our own freedom. John Kennedy's admonition that we would "pay any price, bear any burden, meet any hardship…" in the defense of liberty was not a hollow one. The one unquestionable expense that our country must never shirk from paying is the price to maintain our freedom and to protect our citizens; it is the fundamental reason for which our government exists.

Immoral Purpose

"It's about power and oil," chant the demonstrators. They seldom understand the real issues, and predictably point to convenient and tired slogans. If we wanted oil, we'd take over Mexico, not Iraq! Ditto for the power thing. In reality, the oil was "created" out of U.S. (and British) technology and engineering in the first place, but fair-minded and respectful as we are, we have played along with the oil cartels for decades, allowing their sheiks and princes to become obscenely rich. We would benefit more from developing our own resources, including nuclear and other non-petroleum energy sources of energy. Let the Middle East then wallow in the oil that is of little necessity to us.

What about the others?

Iran, N. Korea and other nations have spawned and supported terror cells, rattled sabers against neighbors, and even threatened America and the free world. It is in our own interest to deal with each of them in ways of our own choosing, and in our own time frame. It is their choice to act in threatening or evil ways; it is our choice of whether, when, and how to respond. It's not that we can't fight battles on more than one front if our nation is threatened; it's that we choose not to. The purveyors of evil in the world know not to test our capacity or our patience. Germany, Japan, and the U.S.S.R. have all offered the world more potential for destructive power than any of the current crop of petty bad guys. These upstarts would be wise to learn from history.

§

CHAPTER 8

FREEDOM

"Necessity is the plea for every infringement of human freedom. It is argument of tyrants. It is the creed of slaves."
~ *William Pitt in the House of Commons November 18, 1783*

INDEPENDENCE DAY (JUN 2003)

Contrary to the modern tendency to commercialize major historical events, we are not celebrating the "4th of July" holiday. We are celebrating its true basis, memorialized in one of the greatest documents ever crafted by human hands: *the Declaration of Independence.* Thomas Jefferson drew up the document in June of 1776, and it was printed during the evening of the 4th of July. Its words should swell the heart of every American, and yet too often they lay dormant with unfamiliarity or forgotten entirely. A periodic reading is required to rekindle an awareness of the great truths embodied within it.

The war of revolution inspired by this awesome call for independence was fueled by desire and depth of conviction; mere munitions could never have prevailed. The result was a constitutional republic that has become the greatest nation on earth; imperfect in many ways, but blessed with the wisdom, courage, and dedication to liberty of its founders. It is the greatest of both irony and tragedy that the independence they sought and achieved has again given way to a level of government dependence that has grown to revolutionary proportions. As we celebrate our independence as a nation, it is time to reassert our independence as individuals.

Gradually, over the past century, our government has usurped the freedom and duty of individuals and families to be personally responsible. Today, life starts with public prenatal care, public transportation to the hospital, publicly assured time-off from work for dad, and even freedom from the responsibility of keeping an unborn child.

As children start their public education, they are given free meals and free day care, relieving many parents from such duties, and furthering dependence on the state.

In driving our kids to school, we are required to use car seats and seat-belts, as another attack on our independence by a government that knows best. It is not the act that offends, it is the surrender of choice.

If we assert our right and duty to provide meals for our own children, there is no end to the label requirements, cautions, and warnings that might befall us; as if we are independent from our own brains.

As kids move along the government run school cycle, they are increasingly indoctrinated with instructions and values that are independent of their parents; and the parents become dependent, willing or not, on the state's instruction in such matters. Sex education, religious values (or lack thereof), political inclinations, attitudes about drugs, and "alternative" lifestyles become matters of the state – not necessarily of our own choosing. Our independent choice of whether to even use public schools is made a costly alternative, and once made, is discouraged, made difficult, or even threatened completely.

If we fail in life, there is a standard to be lowered; if we achieve, there is a tax to be paid. If we don't like our employment or fail to seek it, we can remain dependent on one government program or another to bail us out. The benefits, conditions, and obligations of our employment are all moderated by government regulation to limit even the independence of our choice to stay or go.

We certainly can't be trusted to not overly consume fast food, so the lawyers – and the government – will protect us from that choice. Ditto for smoking, drinking, or riding a motorcycle without a helmet. Our choices are either made for us or strongly encouraged. Alternative choices are either taxed or punished.

Should we make especially poor choices along the way, there are government programs for rehabilitation, therapy, legal defense, and more.

Our later years need not be a worry either, for we have gradually allowed our government to assume responsibility for that too – health care, "retirement" (though the best programs are saved for the government workers and politicians), and our social needs.

Over time, our lack of personal responsibility and freedom has created an evil co-dependence. We are protected and insulated from the negative effects of our bad choices, so we forfeit the ability to make any at all. Emboldened with the success at doing those things from which we derive some measure of benefit, our government extends its reach into more and more, whether we choose them to or not. After all, it's for our protection.

It would seem then, that the greatest gift we can give to honor the independence of our country is to reassert our own.

§

CHAPTER 9

ON THE LIGHTER SIDE

"Humor is perhaps a sense of intellectual perspective: an awareness that some things are really important, others not; and that the two kinds are most oddly jumbled in everyday affairs."
~ Christopher Morley

CONGRESSIONAL ENERGY HEARING (JUN 2008)
The Tables Are Turned - A Sage Exclusive

United States Senators recently held an investigation into the oil industry (in centuries past, these were known as "Inquisitions"). From their royal places seated above and looking down upon the various executives, they lobbed questions designed to embarrass their adversaries and embellish their own standing as defenders of the people.

At the request of the Sierra Sage, an historic re-hearing on the matter was held with the *politicians* questioned by the *oil industry executives*. A table at which all participants were seated at the same level replaced the normally pompous setting. Titles were ignored in an attempt to promote a collegial atmosphere. In attendance were Representative Maxine Waters and Senators Hillary Clinton, Barack Obama, Robert Byrd, Dianne Feinstein and Harry Reid. Representatives of "Big Oil" included executives from Shell Oil, ConocoPhillips, Chevron, BP America and Exxon Mobil.

"Welcome ladies and gentleman," said the head of Shell. "We are hear to discuss obscene oil industry profits and ludicrous executive compensation, with some attention to the energy mess."

Chevron led off with a question for Senator Harry Reid. "Harry, in view of our dependence on foreign oil, yet huge reserves of oil and coal in this country, why have you steadfastly refused to open up our own natural resources and draw on the 250 year supply of coal in our country?"

Reid: "Well, as you know I am a staunch supporter of environmentalists and receive a lot of money – *I mean support* – from them. It's true, we have oil in Alaska, on our ocean shores, in shale and sand in the plains states and in the Gulf. But drilling for oil and gas in our own backyard? Well, there are risks of oil spills and what about the sea lions and starfish? As for coal, well, that's just plain dirty and despite my 30 years in politics, I hate things that are dirty." Let's build windmills – now there is a clean energy source; as clean as the hot air we produce in Congress.

Chevron: "But Senator, isn't there a reason we call them natural *resources*? And with oil likely to reach $200 a barrel, doesn't it make sense to use those resources? We have huge coal reserves and the technology to build very clean plants. And coal is economically viable – wind power takes government subsidies to justify. What about the millions of birds killed flying into windmill farms? And aren't such seas of propellers a scar upon the landscape of our nation?"

Reid: "Well, this is all well and good, but let's talk about your obscene profits!" And by the way, there is no need to discuss the obscene profits on a few of my land deals – none of them have affected my principles in any way! So we lose a few birds; as long as they are right-winged, I don't care.

Exxon Mobil: Dianne, Senators have been critical of the oil company profits and the wealth and earnings of oil company executives. Now, your husband is in the defense contracting business – a hugely profitable business, especially when wars are going on.

Feinstein: That's true. *Is my bow straight?*

Exxon Mobil: And you sat on a Senate Sub-committee that awarded billions of dollars in contracts to your husband's companies, did you not?

Feinstein: Well, yes, but I stepped down from that after it was publicized - so that makes it all ok. *It's not straight, is it?*

Exxon Mobil: Kind of like the fox leaving the hen house – after dinner has been eaten. And, Dianne, your net worth is between 50 and 110 million dollars, assuming your finance reports are accurate. Do you have any questions or comments on *my* income?

Feinstein: Uh.. well…. No. *Damn* this bow!

BP America: Maxine, you recently suggested that the oil industry either come into line with your demands or that they be socialized, did you not? Kind of like Mexico or Venezuela or China or other socialist countries.

Waters: Well… uh.. I didn't REALLY mean that… except that I sort of did. I think profits should be fair and costs should be affordable. If companies can't do that, then the government needs to step in and fix things.

BP America: You mean like they've fixed the energy system itself. Or social security. Or health care. Or education. Or crime and drugs. Or poverty. Maxine, I'm hard pressed in all honesty to find a single thing you people do well!

Waters: What do you mean "you people?" Is that a racist comment? Were you oil people involved in slavery? Just because you're all covered in oil don't mean you have black people workin' there. What color is your secretary, anyway?

BP America: Maxine, getting back to the issue, oil companies do make a lot of money. They also make a lot of investment in R&D and exploration.

They take risks. They produce something of value. And they are rewarded. Now I know those are foreign concepts to those of you in political office. In fact, Exxon Mobil's profits of $9.9 billion in the 3rd quarter of 2005 represented a profit margin of 11%. Microsoft had a margin of 32% and Citigroup was at 33%. Coca-Cola's return was 21%. What is the profit margin on the American people's investment in Congress?

Waters: That's all well and good, but you still made too much money, and we want some. Now, what color is your secretary? How much does she get paid? Oh yes, you know she could be a he! Unless you're a homophobic "stereotyper!"

Byrd: No one's asking me any questions. I've been here 49 years – longer 'an anybody. I think you should name somethin' after me. The Robert Byrd Oil Field or the Robert Byrd Refinery, somethin' like that. Why don't you ask me somethin'? I've been here the longest. Did I say that already? It's time we do somethin' about the cost of energy. In another 50 years I may have somethin'. I need a soda. Does anyone have change?

Obama: Change? Change? I got change. I'm full of change. I'm full of it I tell ya. If you want change, you came to the right place!

Clinton: Everyone is paying attention to Barack. The media is biased. There is a vast right wing conspiracy out there pushing Obama. I need some visibility here! I've got ideas – I'm the smartest woman in America. Rosie O'Donnel says so! Just ask me something. Go ahead.

Shell: Hillary, why don't you come down on trial attorneys and insurance and big real estate firms as you do the oil industry? Oh wait, what's this? A list of top industry political contributors? Hmmm... number 1 is Lawyers - $72 million and you are the largest recipient. The Real estate industry gave $35 million and you, Hillary, were the largest recipient.

Obama: See that – we need change! The audacity of all that corporate money!

Shell: Barack, you got the lion's share of the $51 million retiree industry and also the most from securities and education. That sounds like more of the same – not change. Anyway, back to Hillary. You seem to like taxes. You support windfall profit taxes? Kind of like that $10,000 you parlayed into $100,000 in the commodities market? Actually, isn't your husband's $120 million in speaking and book deals really the ultimate windfall? I mean, he would not have that were he not president. He creates no jobs or wealth for others, only for himself. He contributes nothing for the betterment of mankind or the environment. In fact, one might say his - and Al Gore's - "hot air" contributes to global warming.

Clinton: Well, when we – *I mean he* – was president, the country experienced a great economy. That tremendous run-up in the "dot-com" market was created by our – *I mean his* – presidency. Of course, the "dot-com" bubble burst ... well, that was really George Bush's doing.

Shell: But Hillary, what did you and Bill do in 8 years in the White House and your 8 years in the Senate to deal with the energy needs of the country? Did you push for exploration and drilling? Promote new technologies? *Anything?*

Clinton: No. I think we need to preserve the environment – plus those people give me a lot of money!

Waters: There you go too. What do you mean, "those people?" And by the way, your husband was *not* the first black president!

Clinton: Put a sock in it, my distinguished colleague Ms. Waters. Anyway, as I was saying, we need geothermal, wind and solar – we can call it the "Earth, Wind and Fire" strategy. Of course, those sources need government funding to justify investment. Of course, that will mean government regulation, which in turn will increase costs and require more government subsidies. Nuclear? Now that has possibilities. The Chinese are doing nuclear using our technology. Bill allowed it to be sold to them. Did I tell you the Chinese give Bill and me a lot of money. I mean, it goes to the Library and Foundation. For good causes. Like having the Chinese give us more money.

ConocoPhillips: Well, let's wrap it up with one last question for everyone. What is your position on wind and solar versus oil and nuclear?

Reid: I don't want nuclear storage in Nevada. I don't want coal plants in Nevada – I don't care how clean they are. I'm not making any money off 'em, I don't want 'em. It's George Bush's fault we're in this energy mess anyway. I've been saying that for over 30 years since this mess started. Wait a minute, I've been here 30 years. Could I be part of the problem?

Chevron: That's about the last time we built an oil refinery or nuclear power plant in this country, Harry... about 30 years ago. Thanks for your support.

Feinstein: As long as the contracts are going to my husband's companies, I don't really have an opinion. Can I chair the committee on energy?

BP America: You know, Dianne, your predecessors broke up the Standard Oil monopoly of the Rockefellers in 1911. Since then, you have allowed us to re-monopolize the industry just as you have so many other industries. You really haven't done anything to encourage true competition in the spirit of capitalism. Of course that means much bigger contracts being awarded, more lobbying and political contributions. Wait a minute; I think I'm beginning to understand.

Waters: I like that wind, rain and fire idea. Now, what color is your secretary? Is she Bi? You know you can't discriminate just because she likes women. I think you're racist and sexist *and* homophobic! And you make too much money - more than me!

Byrd: I need a soda. Who's got change? Is somethin' gonna be named after me? I've been here a long, long time. I'm running out of gas myself. Anyone got change?

Reason, Justice and Common Sense

Clinton: Hey Bob – stifle it! First we need to raise taxes. Then we have to enlist volunteers. We'll give them free college if they join our "Clinton Campaign for Energy Improvement" (funded by the Clinton Foundation and the Chinese). We need conservation, so we'll need an agency to monitor consumption. I'll want the files of all those in non-compliance on my desk in the morning. Now Dubai is my husband's partner so they won't count in any changes in oil purchasing. By the way, I'll figure this out – I'm the smartest woman in America.

Obama: I like wind. I use a lot of it - creatively. I use wind to sell change. I use change to sell "wind." Despite that Newton guy, I think perpetual motion has a lot of potential. Jesse Jackson is setting up a new non-profit organization to explore that right now. I like wind though. Besides who cares if we mess up the view of all those spoiled white people living nearby. And why DOES the wind blow mostly in white areas? Is the wind racist? One thing about the wind – if it doesn't blow, you can count on change. And if doesn't change, there is always hope. I hope I've given you a detailed explanation of my position.

Next: *Big Pharma interviews spoiled athletes and movie stars.*

§

A POLITICALLY CORRECT NFL (DEC 2003)

"The National Football League has implemented important policies in the last few years designed to promote minority head coaches throughout the league. For a league that has been dominated for the past two decades by great black athletes, to have so few black coaches is appalling. The current change in policy is the first step in the right direction."
   ~ Kevin M. Yurkerwich, MIT

The season's climax of the NFL was accompanied by the loss or removal of seven head coaches. Minority interest advocates have responded to the search for replacements with demands that more minorities be hired (presumably on the basis that they are "minority," not necessarily the best qualified). This follows decades of complaints that minorities of one group or another are under-represented in the NFL and other sports. Curiously, once many major league sports became dominated by minorities (at least black athletes), the focus shifted to coaches, team executives and owners. As one writer remarked, "Many feel the numbers of coaches and team executives should reflect the number who actually play the game." So if I understand this correctly, it's a problem if participants in a sport don't reflect their composition in the general population, but if they exceed their representation in the general population, then their excess representation should be the standard for other related positions.

It's all very confusing, of course, and defies logic, reason, common sense, and the observed order of things. In an effort to accommodate the ACLU, NAACP, NOW, AARP, NEA, SAG (Screen Actors Guild – they play athletes sometimes), Mexican government, and the newly formed, AOWF (All Other Working Folks), we have proposed a new, improved and politically correct NFL.

(The NBA wasn't considered as it is comprised of 80% black athletes and apparently has a sufficient number of black coaches, trainers, owners, back office staff, front office staff, team masseuses, lawyers, doctors, accountants and financial advisers, so that it is considered racially diverse.)

Now on to the NFL, the diversity of which is just unacceptable. In the remarks that follow, note that general population figures are estimates of current composition, while player percentages are derived from a Northeastern University study based on 1992 data. A cursory survey of teams shows that the 1992 data is reasonably consistent with current make-up of the NFL. Further, considering that there are 32 teams with a typical roster of 64 players, there are a total of 2,048 players in the NFL subject to diversity scrutiny.

U.S. population data shows that we are about 70% White, 12% Black, 13% Latino, 4%, Asian with "all others" about 1%. Figures are difficult to pin down because some people consider themselves more than one group and some, no group. There are other factors besides race to consider as well: sex, age, height, nationality, sexual orientation, and many others. Everyone knows that each of these is indicative of athletic ability and should be considered if we are to truly embrace diversity and equal results.

Applying the population data to the NFL player composition indicates that there is a problem. The NFL is currently 68% Black, 30% White, 1% Hispanic/Latino and 1% Asian. Clearly, a number of black players will have to go and recruitment must be stepped up in the other racial groups. There appears to be a disproportionate number of Samoan players as well. Much work is clearly needed to ensure fair representation of all races.

In addition, 51% must be female (there is currently not a single woman playing in the NFL, if that is not evidence enough of rampant discrimination), while men will be the remaining 49%. Note that 40% of the viewing population is female and that too supports a need for female representation on the field. There is an estimated 3% of the population that is homosexual, though that percentage presumably can be satisfied by either male or female players. Representation among felons appears to be adequate from the news reports over the season and no adjustment is felt necessary. As some felons may be required to serve jail time, recruiting in prisons should, however, be stepped up to ensure proportionate representation on the field.

Another wrinkle is the positional representation. Quarterbacks are especially suspect since they are 94% white. Every one knows that this bias reflects the greater media coverage, higher number of Heisman winners, and just all around glory hogging that quarterbacks get. Of course, 92% of all running backs are black – but that is because they are better at their positions. The same goes for wide receivers (88%), cornerbacks (98%) and defensive backs (95%). Kickers, being kind of a pansy position are not surprisingly 83% white. Clearly, player positions need to be realigned along the same percentages as indicated above.

The average age of NFL players is between 25 and 34 and that group comprises only 14% of the general population. Common sense tells us that those in the 0-15 range and those in the 75-85+ ranges are probably unsuitable for the NFL. But there are lots of active people in other age groups. To be fair, the composition should include 16% in the 35-44 bracket, 15% in the 45-54 bracket, 10% in the 55-64 bracket, and 6.5% in the 65-74 group (the last group perhaps skewed a bit toward the kicking position).

While there are a number of smokers and drinkers in the general population, there is little sympathy for their proportional inclusion in the NFL; they will, however, be tolerated (smoking and drinking will not be allowed on the field, in the parking lots, in the locker room, or in the stands). Drug and steroid use appears adequately represented.

The issue of height and weight is not considered a flagrant violation of diversity standards since there appear to be lots of tall, skinny players and more than a few "plus sized" ones. Still, the truly "little people" lack a presence as do those differently enabled. Certainly opportunities exist as holders for the extra point kicks that could be filled by those who are height challenged.

The issue of religious affiliation should be addressed to avoid hurt feelings – these are very sensitive people after all. Some groups have remarked that handling a "pigskin" football is offensive to their beliefs and some sort of synthetic alternative should be used in the spirit of unity. As a majority, Christians need no special attention, and in fact should do the Christian thing and step aside to make places for other religions. If there is any team prayer, it must be said in all religious formats, to all known deities, and in all languages represented on the team (which, if the team is truly diversified, will include all languages). Terrorism spawned by religious or other beliefs will not be tolerated on or off the field. *There are limits.*

Out of respect for PETA, teams may not use animal names, no matter how regal or elegant sounding some may insist they are; we all know that such branding is offensive to the animal. Rocks, flowers, and landmarks are lovely alternatives. The Pittsburgh Petunias has a nice ring.

In solidarity with the rights of all workers, pay will be uniform throughout the new NFL, with adjustments for seniority only. Players will be expected to share in the team profits (but not losses). Performance, afterall, is simply not a valid basis for adjustment in pay.

So there you have it – the New, Politically Correct NFL.

Obviously, the real issues in professional athletics are capability and performance; and the real goal should be access, not outcome. If a sport, a position or a job function is dominated by a particular group of individuals, it is likely because they are better or more qualified at what they do. Numerical representation is a silly notion, and the sooner we drop that whole charade, the better off we will all be. We'll also be better off when we pay more attention to what we have in common, and less to that which may be different. If Blacks dominate the running game, so be it – just so long as an Asian, Hispanic, or White guy can try out. The same is true for coaching – and believe me, if a coach can win 12-14 games in a season, no owner is going to reject him because of the color of his skin. It's time we lost the numerical representation mind set and got on with football – and life.

§

TEN HEADLINES WE WISH WE'D SEEN IN 2003 (JAN 2004)

"To the press alone, checkered as it is with abuses, the world is indebted for all the triumphs which have been gained by reason and humanity over error and oppression."
  ~ James Madison

WAR ON TERRORISM SUCCEEDS

Buoyed by the striking success of the U.S led war on terrorism, France, Germany, and Canada joined the international coalition against evil, forging a complete alliance in support of peace. Following the actions of Libya, rogue nations and dictators around the world have begun laying down their arms, opening their countries to inspection, and prosecuting and surrendering terrorist groups all over the globe. France joined the U.S., U.K., and Israel in taking out Iran's nuclear facilities.

U.N. REPLACED

In a unanimous vote, both house of Congress voted to withdraw from the cranky, egotistical, and bureaucratic United Nations. NATO nations have agreed to a gradual replacement of this aging alliance, and leading nations in the world have agreed to the formation of an organization summit to create new bodies for the purpose of securing world peace, fostering international relations, and preserving the rights of free states.

NATIONALISM CURBED - STATES RIGHTS RESTORED

President Bush has tackled the issue of rampant nationalism with a bold program to return the fed to its limited and constitutionally mandated role, and restore the rights and duties of states envisioned by the founders. He has issued executive orders for the orderly dismantling of most cabinet offices and their associated departments. He has convened a special conference of Governors to establish plans for the gradual transfer of functions and revenues, to be managed at the state level. The days of federal pork and bloated bureaucracy are over, and a return to state responsibility and local control is on the horizon. (See related story on Taxation.)

IRS ABOLISHED; TAX SYSTEM SCRAPPED

In a rare display of collective sanity, the president and Congress have agreed to abolish the IRS and the entire perverted system of taxation under which the country has suffered for the past 90 years! A new, simplified system will be instituted comprised of a single sales tax to be administered at the state level. The system will provide for no individual, corporate, or non-profit exceptions and will only involve limited and equitable exemptions. The new tax system will be coupled with a federal cap on spending tied to GDP, and states are encouraged to enact similar limits tied to Gross State Production. Model state legislation is being developed and will be encouraged for adoption. A five-year phase-in will allow for minimal disruption of employment in tax related industries and government employment, which is expected to drop considerably at all levels.

ALLIANCES RENEWED

Americans have come to the realization that the people in alliance countries are not necessarily of the same opinion as their leadership. In a similar manner, citizens of these long-standing allies have come to realize that the U.S. is not the bully and bad guy portrayed by their own more liberal advocates, but in fact is the world's best friend. With the decline of terrorism in the world, many in Paris have taken to wearing cowboy hats.

NEW IMMIGRATION SYSTEM

A 5-year moratorium on immigration has been implemented and a blue ribbon commission established to review and implement a sweeping new program for the country. Goals have been established based on a proposal first announced in a small, monthly Nevada magazine, the Sierra Sage.

NEVADA SUPREME COURT ACTS

Responding to the deadlock in the Nevada Legislature over spending and taxing, the Nevada Supreme Court exhibited both simplicity and wisdom. A unanimous court agreed to respect the will of the people and keep the State Constitution intact by ordering the immediate implementation of the prior biennium budget. The Governor, they advised, is within his power to continue to call the legislature into special session to pass a new budget, respecting the requirement for a 2/3 majority for any new taxes. Education and other government functions will be funded at the prior budget levels in the interim. Bureaucrats have been advised to "just deal with it."

NATION UNDER GOD AFFIRMED
The Supreme Court affirmed that this is indeed "one nation, under God." The majority cited volumes of historical documentation, beginning with the first voyages to America. The guarantee of freedom of religion, they concluded, was in fact consistent with the well-established beliefs of the nation. They reasserted that the nation, and in fact the court itself, were elements of a government established under rights granted people by God – not by government. They reasoned perfectly that the right of a government to establish a government was, in fact, a contradiction in terms. Thank God.

LEGISLATURE LIMITS LAWS
Nevada led the nation in the new trend of legislatures actually reducing the number of laws. Recognizing that we are a nation of too many laws, our elected leaders resolved to commit the entire session to the reduction, simplification and consolidation of existing laws. As a result of the historic session, the state will begin 2004 with 352 *fewer* laws on the books. Legislators and citizens alike were so enthralled that a contest is being proposed to see which legislator can reduce the greatest number of laws! Other states and the federal government are expected to follow suit.

TOLERANCE URGED
The major media discovered new beneficiaries of tolerance: the English speaking, white European men, heterosexuals and Christians. In a similar effort to fully embrace diversity, many newspapers and universities are now actively recruiting journalists and professors with a conservative orientation. *Ben Franklin is smiling.*

§

CHAPTER 10

PERSONAL REFLECTIONS

"There are two distinct classes of what are called thoughts: those that we produce in ourselves by reflection and the act of thinking, and those that bolt into the mind of their own accord"
    ~ Thomas Paine

A CHRISTMAS APOLOGY (DEC 2005)

As we enter the Christmas season, I realize I have been guilty of many transgressions over the past year, and will likely be guilty of them in the next and in those to follow. I have therefore decided to come clean with a complete admission of guilt - and to apologize for my sins and errors.

Of course, my first apology must be for simply being a Christian and recognizing Christmas as such. Many, in their zeal to avoid causing discomfort to anyone (other than Christians) will avoid the use of such an inflammatory term and resort to more innocuous ones such as "Season's Greetings," "Happy Holidays" or even "The best to you on your choice of holy day or other event which gives you pleasure during this blustery time of year." No, *it is Christmas* – and it is a time for celebration of the birth of Jesus Christ. That is appropriate in a country with an culture that was founded on traditions rooted in Christian philosophy.

I apologize for not shopping at those stores who haven't the guts to rise above political correctness and therefore instruct employees to avoid the use of the term "Christmas." Note to those merchants in this category: your decision to not offend any other special group has offended 85% of the country who are Christians and whose own great tolerance you have repaid with intolerance for their heritage.

A belief in the greatness of America seems to hold little favor among many liberals at home and abroad. Our valiant efforts to rid the world of terrorists and to secure freedom for so many are met with derision and disdain from Hollywood, academia, and the mainstream media. So to those misguided souls, I issue an apology for believing that America is the greatest country on earth, and the greatest hope for the future of all mankind.

For those who think that families are obsolete and that two moms, two dads or a cross-dressing commune are all comparable alternatives, I apologize. For you see, I still hold the quaint notion that we are created as men and women for a purpose; and that men and women come together as couples and to create families for a purpose; and that families assemble into communities for a purpose. I understand that some may hold different views – they are not evil for doing so; they are simply wrong. Nonetheless, I apologize for thinking differently.

I apologize for thinking that the purpose of education is to enlighten and expand the minds of those assimilated into a single and unique American culture; a culture molded from western European traditions, in which the language of English is a common bond, and with equal opportunity, not equal outcome, the fundamental message of equality.

To those who feel entitled to feed on the efforts, risks, and investment of others, I apologize. You see it seems to me that the grant of freedom and opportunity to pursue our dreams carries with it a duty of personal responsibility, and acceptance of the outcomes of our efforts.

To those who fail to understand the difference between humans and lower animals, I apologize. I understand that you may prefer to dine on sunflower seeds and petunia petals in celebration of the "Winter Holiday." I, on the other hand, expect to fully partake in the bounty provided by nature's God – including prime rib! So if that bothers you, I apologize.

Christmas is a time of wonder, a time of thanks, and a time of reflection.

In celebrating the wonder of Jesus Christ, we are all humbled. In appreciation for Him as God's gift to humanity, we are all thankful. In our attempts to understand the meaning of all life on earth, we should all reflect on our lives and the world around us.

To be sure, the burdens are daunting and the challenges to our minds and hearts huge. I will continue in the new year to try to understand in ways that I can, and I will try to share my interpretations with others. I don't expect to be right, or even necessarily agreed with – but I will do my best, and for that, I make no apology.

THE COWBOY LIFE (JUN 2008)
An American Metaphor

"I ain't got a dime, but what I got is mine; I ain't rich but Lord I'm free."
    ~ *From the George Strait song, "Amarillo By Morning"*

I had the pleasure of going on the Reno Rodeo Cattle Drive recently - my 8th such event. They have all been fun, but this one seemed to inspire a bit more reflection; perhaps because it may be my last (tough on the old knees); or perhaps because I simply paid more attention to those things less obvious. In any event, it occurred to me that the reason for the timeless popularity of the cowboy way of life is that it represents America. It is a metaphor for the American way of life - *at least what it used to be.*

Hollywood notwithstanding, the "cowboy era" was a brief period in American history. It lasted from about 1850 to 1890. It was propelled by the gold rush in the West and a newly discovered national demand for beef. It lasted only until the advent of the railroad and barbed wire fencing across formerly open lands cut it short. In those days, cowboys would herd cattle hundreds of miles, 15 miles a day, moving perhaps 3,000 head with 10 cowboys and 4-5 horses each. The cowboy life is still alive today, but limited. Many are involved with "regular" jobs while some still work ranches, or rodeo. All share the same values. American values.

Independence
A month after the drive, we celebrate our Declaration of Independence. Cowboys take that seriously. Independence is a hallmark of their lives. Cowboy independence is not about being alone; it's about choosing with whom you spend your time. It's about *socializing* as you choose to, not *socialism* in which someone else chooses for you. It's about being who you are, not someone you're supposed to be. It's about taking risks – or not – because you choose to.

Some years ago on the cattle drive, a number of us standing in line at a lunch stop were startled to hear a whoop and a holler from high above the sheer mountain face that was our morning backdrop. There atop the sheer slope was Cecil Jones astride his horse. Cecil was a member of the Cowboy Hall of Fame – and 82-years-old. To the delight and amazement of the crowd below, not to mention a bit of terror, Cecil gave his horse a jerk on the reins and started straight down the slope, zigging and zagging and kicking up rocks and dust. He wasn't showing off; he was celebrating the right to be free. It was an incredible sight, and an even more incredible lesson in life about freedom.

Happiness

If freedom is essential for the perfection of man, then happiness is its first object. The Founders had it right: "life, liberty, and the pursuit of happiness." Of course, there is happiness in simply being independent and free, but that also allows for the pursuit of higher objectives. Cowboys are happy because they are simple. They don't need a lot of trappings to add fulfillment to their lives. A good bedroll can make one just as happy as a million dollar RV – it's just a matter of perspective. When I was a kid growing up, people could be happy in a small but warm home, with a family car and little else. Today, a 5,000 SF house and 2 BMWs in the garage don't produce the same level of content. Kids have their own television, computer, cell phone, video game, and the latest clothing - and yet seem miserable. The cowboy understands why.

Toughness/Kindness

The same cowboy riding a 2,000 pound bull can just as easily be cradling an infant son in loving arms. The kind of toughness that will fight to protect family and property, will just as easily become the strength to help a fallen friend to his feet or a neighbor rebuild his home. You see, in the world of the cowboy, it's not about being tough; it's about being strong. True strength is not about power - it is about character.

Interestingly, for all the hoops we jump through these days to ensure equal rights and opportunity for women, cowgirls don't seem to notice (nor do they take offense at the term cowgirl). They saddle their own horses, they buck hay and muck stalls; they can ride, rope and do most anything else. They ask for no special accommodation or preference. They exhibit naturally the kind of equality that so many others insist must be accorded to them by law. For all their "toughness," they maintain the loving kindness of the mothers and mates they most often are. Feminists could take a lesson.

Self-reliance

A wagon train rolls along with the cattle drive, guided by teams of elegant draft horses and mules, and piloted by hard-working "teamsters." The wagons are as majestic as the beasts that pull them. One problem: if a wheel comes off or an axle or rein breaks, they can't call down to the local auto supply. They carry tools, and knowledge – and the self-reliance that characterizes their world - the world of the cowboy.

These folks don't ask for or even want a "bail-out" from some government agency when things don't go their way. They often don't have much, but what they have is theirs – and their responsibility. If something lacks a purpose, they don't need it; if it comes with strings attached, they don't want it. I wonder what life in the ghetto would be like if we turned it into a corral?

Respect

Cowboys tip their hat to a lady; they call a man they just met "Sir." It's not quaint; it's who they are. They are taught this by lesson and by example from the time they are young. Listen to some country music; now listen to some "Rap" or "Heavy Metal." Do you think there might be some connection? I don't recall ever hearing a country song that included the term "ho."

Respect is taught young in cowboy life, as it should be in all walks of life. By the time a person is 5 or 6-years-old, they either have it or they don't. Respect for life comes from being around animals at an early age and learning the responsibilities we have to them – a respect for life in all forms. Respect is taught for God and country; for the elderly and the infirm; for women; for those in authority. It's such a simple concept, and yet seemingly few have much of it. It's rare in society generally, but pretty much commonplace in the cowboy world.

God-loving

When you go on a cattle drive, you sign a waiver of liability acknowledging that you may be "injured, permanently maimed, or killed." In other words, along with your personal duty to pay attention to what you are doing, you are in God's hands.

There was an occasion on this year's cattle drive when one of the staff cowgirls took a spill from her horse. Being an excellent rider it was unexpected; but then cowboys are taught to expect the unexpected. It might have been faintness from low blood sugar. She hit her head when she fell – always a concern - and was taken to the hospital by helicopter. On the news of the accident, we were all gathered together and we did something we don't do much in public these days. We were led in prayer. We prayed for her safety and return to health, and in thankfulness for our own continued safety and good health.

Toward the end of the drive, another staff member was catching up to the herd in a lope when his horse stepped into a soft anthill and he was thrown. He wasn't hurt in the fall - typical cowboy toughness – but as the horse struggled to right itself, one of its hooves caught the cowboy dangerously in the head. Fellow cowboys, including medics, rushed to his aid and he was covered in blood. They tended to him as they could and called for the Care Flight which arrived quickly. He was taken to the hospital. Again, we came together in prayer. He was back that night.

Cowboys aren't so much God-fearing people as they are God-loving. Their work world is among God's earth and amidst all His creations. They have a respect for nature's God that was typical of our Founders, and they seek his divine presence in times of need. All they have on earth is wondrous, but they know there are times when their eyes and hearts must be lifted to the sky. They make no apology for their beliefs.

Family
There were husbands and wives on the this last cattle drive, as there had been before. There was a mother and her grown son, and a father and his. There were sisters and brothers and friends. When guests and staff returned from their week of western adventure, they were greeted at the Rodeo grounds by spouses and kids, friends and relatives. The only thing unusual about this was that it was so typical.

Cowboys aren't insulated from the troubles and tragedies that afflict families, but they seem uncommon in how they cling to the noble tradition of family structure and stability. They eat together. They ride together. They talk together. While family is at the center of the cowboy life, extended family is prized as well; there's always a seat at the table.

Common Sense
Most cowboys will tell you they don't know much. That's probably more humility than truth. Cowboys that I have known have an abundance of knowledge, including common sense. Common sense comes from just paying attention to the world around you, and since cowboys spend more time in that world, they seem to get a better dose of it than most. Kids might be better off with less time watching "reality" television and more time enjoying the true reality of the cowboy world.

Patriotism
At the start of each Reno Rodeo lineup, a group of about 20 young girls rides into the arena. These aren't just any young girls. They are top horse-women: sweet, smart, innocent, and hard working. They volunteer and pay the costs of their participation. When they come riding into the arena, they have an American flag in one hand, a pair of reins in the other, and a 1,200 pound animal beneath them. They come in at a full gallop; fearless, smiling, and proud. They are as much a symbol of America as the banner they carry. Between the thunderous response to them entering the arena, the saluting of Old Glory, and the singing of the National Anthem, there is

little doubt as to the patriotic feelings of this crowd. There is not a hat on anyone's head; it's over their hearts. There is hardly a dry eye. But there is an overflowing of pride in their nation: a God loving, independent, family oriented, hard-working, tough, caring, kind, and giving nation.

There's a simple reason for this: cowboys don't just love America, they *are* America. The values of the cowboy are the values that America has held since its founding. Much of the country has misplaced those values, but as long as cowboys sit in the saddle and ride free, those values will never be without a home.

§

GIVING
Is an American tradition in danger? *(DEC 2008)*

"The only way to be loved is to be and to appear lovely; to possess and display kindness, benevolence, tenderness; to be free from selfishness and to be alive to the welfare of others."
    ~ John Jay

It was sometime in the 1950s. I was about ten years old and each Saturday, Dad would take me and my younger brother grocery shopping. It was always quite an event, David pushing one shopping-cart and me the other, as Dad filled the carts with an assortment of meats, cheese, milk and various other stuff. We were a family of seven, and often had "extended family" or friends as dinner guests, so the pantry and freezer were always well stocked.

A Mexican couple was in front of us as we navigated the aisles, accompanied by two girls a bit younger than my brother and me. Dad noticed the woman pick something off the shelf and look to the husband. Often he would shake his head "no," and she would return the item to the shelf. As we moved to the register, the couple and their two girls were still in front of us, our carts filled to the brim while theirs was meagerly so.

My dad grew up during the Depression, and was one of 16 kids. His folks were dairy farmers, and despite the large family, there was always food on the table, mostly home grown or raised, with soups and bread as a staple. I think that was one reason my dad always had a soft spot for the hungry – especially kids. On many Thanksgivings, my mom and dad would spend a day shopping, fill about 30 bags with turkeys and trimmings and drive a pickup truck to one of the poor neighborhoods. There, they would pass out to people on the street these simple gifts in appreciation for our own family blessings. The gracious smiles and nods of appreciation were their reward.

As we moved forward toward the checkout register, my dad took the man by the arm and gently pulled him aside. "I noticed as you were shopping, your wife would take things from the shelves and ask about them and then put them back. Are you out of work?' The man held his head high but replied, "Yes, for the moment. We just need to watch things a bit." My dad looked at the girls and reached for his wallet. "Here, take this," he said, handing the man a $100 dollar bill. "Take this. I want you to go back and get everything you put back on the shelves and put it in your basket… for the kids." "No," the man protested, "thank you, but I can't accept this." "It's ok – it's not a gift," said Dad, aware of the stranger's pride, "it's a loan. Here's my business card. I'm a builder here in town. Come and see me Monday. You have a job."

On Monday, the stranger showed up and went to work for my dad as a construction laborer. He returned the $100 from his first paycheck and continued to work for Dad for a number of years. He was hardworking, determined and bright – attending college in the evenings to study engineering. He rose over the years to become a carpenter, foreman, and finally, superintendent. He also obtained his college degree.

He came to my dad one day with a look of concern and said," Leonard, I appreciate all you have done for me but I have to leave. I've been offered a very good job in engineering with a big firm in Mexico, and I think I should return to accept it." My dad smiled: "Bill, it's been great having you here but you need to follow your dreams and opportunities. Take the job. We'll stay in touch."

Bill, his wife Adele, and their two daughters returned to Mexico and he went to work for the large manufacturer of electrical products. Our families did stay in touch over the years, and one day we got a phone call letting us know that Guiellermo "Bill" Maldonado had been appointed Chairman of the Board of Square D Corporation International. The simple gesture in a grocery years earlier store began a cycle of friendship and success that I have always remembered and treasured. It was but one small example of the wondrous power of giving.

Americans are giving people; it's one of the defining characteristics of an American. We are blessed with much and find joy in sharing with others in need. When someone suffers a tragedy, or experiences a loss, people from all walks and stations of life reach out to give as they can. From children to seniors, Americans open their hearts and wallets to help when disaster strikes or emergencies arise. They feed the hungry, offer clothing and shelter to those in need, and rebuild both property and lives when they are broken, with nothing ever expected in return. Americans give at the highest levels, often with their lives, to protect their way of life, and to pave the road to freedom for others a world apart.

Something has changed, however. Many have become cynical or jaded about giving. Recipients in need have too often become "victims," exhibiting a sense of entitlement rather than appreciation. Large "charitable" organizations have displaced more personal giving, and are staffed with highly paid executives living lives of opulence and privilege, in stark contrast to those they "serve." Government has seen fit to deny individuals the gift of giving, instead confiscating from them to give to others as *it* chooses, and its choices are often questionable. Giving is fundamentally a voluntary act; that is what makes it special. It is also personal. The pleasure of giving is in the thankful smile or grateful tears of those who benefit from simple acts of kindness. When a distant bureaucracy takes involuntarily from one for the invisible use by another, it is not giving, it is theft.

CEOs of local and regional non-profit agencies around the country make an average of around $160,000 annually, with other senior staff also very well paid. The national head of the Boys & Girls Clubs of America was paid $557,013 in 2007 with many others paid similar compensation. In addition, many charitable groups pay out far more in administration and salaries than is directed to their "cause." Such behaviors make many less inclined to contribute - not just to these organizations, but to give at all.

In the case of government "giving" the matter is even worse. The most egregious violation, of course, is that money is not "given" by taxpayers, but confiscated from them and then doled out to favored groups at home and abroad. Citizens have no choice as to whether their money is given to some Third World country (often enriching corrupt leaders), ACORN "community activists," or some other government-determined cause. People regularly gouged in this manner by their elected representatives become angry and less likely to care about causes more deserving and closer to them.

Giving to others in need is truly its own reward. Millions of Americans give of their time and finances in small ways and large every day. They are motivated by nothing more than kindness and caring for fellow human beings. God bless them all. They understand that the real answer to genuine need lies in the human spirit, not in government bureaucracies or bloated institutions. In a time when many seem to think that more government is the answer to everything, we risk undermining that spirit.

Our right to pursue happiness includes the right to give freely of ourselves to others as we see fit – it does not include the right of government to take involuntarily from us as it deems entitled.

§

A FATHER'S WORDS (MAY 2003)

"When I was a boy of 14, my father was so ignorant I could hardly stand to have the old man around. But when I got to be 21, I was astonished at how much the old man had learned in seven years."
    ~ Mark Twain

My dad passed away January 12, 1999. I miss him every day, but on Father's Day, it's especially important to remember some of the lessons I learned from him; lessons similar, I imagine, to those learned by many sons and daughters.

Dad was fond of sayings – some he'd heard, some he made up along the way, but in a few words he was a master at translating a philosophy born of simple values and universal applicability. Some of those expressions "went in one ear, and out the other," though years later they'd revisit me and generate a fuller understanding and a smile. I'd like to share a few of them, together with a little better interpretation that has come from my own years of reflection.

"I can do anything a small man can do except for one thing – he can go through a smaller hole."

My father was a building contractor – a big man in stature, with a bit of a booming nature that befit his vocation. When he spoke in his trademark expressions, it was usually accompanied by a raised eyebrow or a laugh – and if he really liked you, a slap on the shoulder. When I was a kid, this remark drew a laugh. As I grew older, I realized the deeper message in what he had said, and it was this: a person can do most anything, save that for which he or she is physically limited from doing. That is an incredible message. Coupled with the freedom we enjoy as Americans, we are restricted only by our physical limits - and our own choices.

"It doesn't cost one dime to be nice to someone."

Why open a door for someone? Or give up a chair? Or stop to let a car merge into traffic. Or do anything that takes so little on our part to make someone else a little more comfortable, a little more charmed, or to simply impart a smile. After all, it really doesn't cost you even a dime. Manners, common courtesy, and civility are all so easy to give – but they seem so hard to find.

"Who's smarter, you are the kid?"

I was about 13 or 14 and occasionally went along with my dad at Saturday breakfasts with some of his subcontractors. One time, one of the gentlemen asked about my future plans and I told him I planned to go to college. On hearing that he turned to my dad and asked: "So Leonard, who's smarter – you or the kid?" Without hesitation, my dad replied with a laugh: "He is - I've taught him everything I know, and he damn well better learn something on his own." There is an important lesson in that quip: each succeeding generation should improve upon its predecessor. This assumes, of course, that the earlier generation passes on its knowledge and experience – and that the succeeding generation makes some measure of contribution.

"If you can read, you can do anything."

One of sixteen children born to Portuguese immigrant dairy farmers, my dad did not have the opportunity for much formal education. He was a bright man, however, and very self motivated. He relished knowledge and knew that much could be found in books. He passed on that inclination to his children both by his example, and in his homespun advice. I have come to adopt that sage advice and truly believe it.

"No one ever died of hard work."

Some will differ and claim that someone has "worked himself to death." I'm inclined to believe my father's characterization. If one works within his or her capabilities but reaches beyond their grasp, both the satisfaction and the achievement will be rewarding. Of course, it's important to take time to love, give, share, and enjoy the other pleasures in life. My dad was blessed to consider his work almost a hobby – I'm equally blessed.

"No one ever said 'life's fair.' "

When things don't go as planned or desired, we are tempted these days to lodge a complaint, file a lawsuit, or grumble forever after about how we got the short end of the stick. We would do well, instead, to accept that simple saying – and move on. The time spent trying to right a perceived wrong is better spent pursuing a new endeavor – and often, the "wrong" wasn't much of one anyway!

"If my sons are half as good as the old man, they'll be good men."

This was always one of my favorites. It sounds boastful, but it was never said with the slightest degree of ego. Rather, it was said with a hearty laugh, a wink, and a subtle challenge. "Hey," he was saying, "I've done my part. I've met the challenges of a depression, a world war, a limited education, a large immigrant family, and more. It's worked out pretty well. Your challenge is to do better." It always has been a challenge. You see, Dad was a big man; but more than that, he was a *great* man. I'd be proud to be half the man he was.

Happy Father's Day, Dad – the messages aren't forgotten, though the lessons are still being learned.

§

A MESSAGE TO MY TEACHERS
Thank You *(OCT 2003)*

"He that teaches us anything which we knew not before is undoubtedly to be reverenced as a master."
~ Samuel Johnson

I recently heard of the passing of one of my former high school teachers, Mr. Bob Wright. I had Mr. Wright for chemistry, and like many former teachers, I owe a great debt of gratitude to him. With his passing, I'm reminded that the time is long overdue to pay public tribute to the many teachers who have profoundly affected my life, and the lives of countless others, as many teachers have done and continue to do. This is a thank you to some of those teachers. Though I have learned much from many, a few stand out for special lessons learned.

Grade School
Mrs. Singer – Kindness
By 3rd grade, we were getting into some pretty serious academics. Mom was PTA president around that time, so kids in our family were well known to all our teachers. I was a bit of a handful – reasonably smart and responsible, capable of boredom, and a bit independent. Mrs. Singer was always so gracious, kind and attentive though, so no one – not even me – would let her down. She inspired kindness by showing her own – always.

Mrs. Zimmer – Encouragement
I had Mrs. Zimmer for both 5th and 6th grades. She was a lovely lady, a bit cherubic, with a fondness for polka-dot dresses. She had the kids in her class all participate in the "Yum-Yum Club" wherein each of us would cook or bake some delicacy each week to be shared with the rest of the class. It was fun – and my inspiration to continue to experiment with cooking to this day. My performance could have been a bit better at times, and sensing a little frustration with the speed of things, she encouraged me to do independent projects. Work became a little more fun, and performance became a little more in line with capabilities.

Mr. Rudy Buchser – Discipline

Mr. Buchser was part of a family of educators, including a brother I would later have for Geometry, and his father, who was the School District Superintendent. He was the middle school principal, and not a man to be messed with. In those days, the principal had a paddle in his office – and used it. More than one wayward truant or "garbage mouth" found himself on the business end of the paddle, and the wails coming from the principal's office were enough to keep the rest of us mindful of our duties. Despite the role I doubt he ever relished, he was always a fair-minded and great guy – and a great example.

High School

Mr. Bob Buchser – Humor

I had Geometry as a freshman with Bob Buchser, having taken Algebra I in the 8th grade. Most of the other kids were sophomores, and were a little more socially advanced than a gawky freshman. Mr. Buchser was well aware of this – and treated us no differently, despite that obvious handicap. What he did do was make things fun. In between angles, theorems, and proofs, there was always a joke or a chuckle. A lot of tough things are less so, I learned, when taken with a smile. I had the pleasure of quietly picking up a dinner check some years later as I ran into Mr. Buchser and his wife at a local restaurant. It was nice to repay the smiles in a small way.

Miss Dossee – Precision

My sister had her for several years of both English and Latin, so I was well prepared for this taskmaster of language, literature and Latin - *I thought*. My sister was one of her favorites, thereby posing an insurmountable challenge for her younger sibling. Miss Dossee, I'm afraid, expected a lesser student, and I did not disappoint her. She never married, except to her profession – teaching was her life, and she lived it fully. She regaled in reading *Beowolf* with a Gaelic accent that made the imponderable work even more so. She set perfection as the only goal, and when one thinks about it, had the goal been mediocrity, it would surely have been achieved. Whatever interest I have in reading, and whatever skills I have in writing and communicating, I owe to that woman. I still fall short of excellence – but it remains my goal.

Miss Gannon – Caring

She was fresh out of college. I think we were her first history class - her trial… by fire. Having made it past my freshman year, I was a bit smug – no, smart aleckie! She was a great teacher and planted a fondness for history I retain today. She was always caring. There was one time though, in a non-stop display of "goofing off" in class, she pulled me aside for a good – and well deserved – talking to. I don't know if it was the stress of the day, or my antics that brought her to a few tears. Boy, did I feel badly. I'm pretty sure I apologized somewhere along the way, but just in case – "I am so sorry, Miss Gannon."

Mr. Polk and Mr. Taylor – Coolness

They had only been out of college a couple of years, but had a classy confidence that made them light years ahead in knowledge and wisdom. They never flaunted it. They were always cool. They were careful not to be too chummy with their students, but in their personalities and style, were never too distant from them either. They were cool in a classy, professional way – and still are. I saw them both at a local wedding of mutual friends. I call them Buck and Jim now. That's pretty cool.

Mr. Giles – Hard Work

Dean Giles was my varsity basketball coach – when I made the varsity team the second time around. Mr. Giles used to jokingly refer to our team as "small but slow" – and he could have easily been talking about me, but he wasn't. He called me aside when I first tried out – not to tell me I wasn't good enough, but to tell me that I was. I just didn't work hard enough. He was right. So I worked harder and made the team. Oh, I still wasn't that good, but the lesson of working hard was worth more in my life than the game itself.

Mr. Bordenave and Mr. Dougherty – Stability

Mr. Bordenave was built like a little bear; Mr. Dougherty (an All-American at Santa Clara University in its Orange Bowl heyday) was built like a big one. They were the vice-principal and principal, respectively. They were rocks. Nothing got by them. If you got in a little trouble, you didn't want to have to face these two. So you pretty much stayed out of trouble.

College
Fr. Coz – Humanity
Father Coz was a regular guy. He was more of a counselor and a friend to students than an Economics professor, though he was both. I enjoyed him greatly as a friend. For years following graduation from Santa Clara University, I would get a Christmas card from him. Even after five or six moves, even throughout my time in the military, somehow, he would find me – and send a card. Pure kindness and humanity. I would see him occasionally over the years – he never forgot my name, nor anyone else's to my recollection.

Fr. Fagothey – Ethics
He literally wrote the book. We used a text on Ethics bearing his name, and studied something profoundly fundamental to any true education: *right and wrong.* I would go through life doing a few things right, and too many wrong – but always mindful of the difference. Like most of philosophy, the essence is not in the doing; it is in the knowing. He taught us to know – the doing was up to us.

Dr. Barker – Perseverance
I guess by now I'd forgotten some of Coach Giles' message, and was not working especially hard to master Physics. As a pre-med student though, that was not a good thing. Sensing the problem, Dr. Barker asked me to retake his course. With fatherly counsel, he told be to get off my butt and work harder. If the assignment called for working half the problems at the end of the chapter, work all of them. If we were required to master material for an exam in 5 days, master it in 3 – and then review it again. I did. It worked. I got an A the second time around... and learned more than Physics.

Dr. Fast – Wisdom

Dr. Fast *wasn't*. He was slow and easy going; always having time for any question from any student. His schedule seemed to be what you required, not what *he* did. His steady pace and insight into students needs worked. Students learned and many went on to pursue advanced science or medical studies - I wasn't one of them, though not for lack of encouragement from Tom Fast. He mentioned something to me one day that struck me as no less than profound. He said, " You don't go into medicine to study science, you do it to help people – and there are lots of paths to doing that." He told me something that likely reflected his own life, and was a wonderful guide to mine - or anyone else's.

Dr. Trickett – Imagination

Joe Trickett taught management – the art of getting things done through people. He was a master and taught me the importance of thinking outside the box before "thinking outside the box" became popular. I learned that dreaming is as powerful as knowing, perhaps more so.

Dean Dirksen – Elegance

"Charlie" Dirksen started the MBA program at Santa Clara, and was highly respected in both business circles and academia. He was always approachable, and yet carried himself with grace and elegance wherever he was. He was a great example of being heard while speaking softly. He garnered admiration not for who he was, but for the kind of person he was.

I could share more about most every teacher I have ever had. The vast majority were great teachers – knowledgeable, professional, kind, caring, and great examples. I have not always exemplified the lessons I learned from them, though the lessons are there. At the end of my life, I hope I will not have squandered the wisdom they instilled. If I do, it will not be because I was not taught. So I thank them, each of them, for more than simply knowledge – but for lessons in life.

§

FIFTY YEARS AGO... (DEC 2005)

"It is, I believe, the greatest generation any society has ever produced."
  ~ *Tom Brokaw*

Fifty years ago education taught, health care healed, families shared, businesses – big and small - worked, public services assisted, and charities cared. Going into 2006, it is more and more clear than none of these work any more, and there is a common thread: *government.*

One wants to begin the New Year on a note of optimism, but optimism which ignores reality is either naiveté or wishful thinking. The point of this commentary is not to dwell on the bleakness that exists, nor to pretend that it doesn't, but to remind us of a greatness that was – and can be again, if we deal with the root cause of decline.

Public education in the 1950s-60s produced a societal intellect that built space ships, computers, televisions, and much of the modern technology we enjoy today. The advances in health and science were outcomes of this educational model. The model was simple: students, teachers, and parents; a focus on solid academics; and performance standards. What was absent was the influence of government, bureaucrats, and unions. The education-al curriculum was geared toward fundamental knowledge and teaching methodology was simple, experientially validated, and teacher driven. The result was excellence among those with the highest levels of capability, while those of more modest abilities left at least with a diploma and the basic knowledge to perform as good citizens.

The heavy hand of government, unions and bureaucracy has driven out many outstanding teachers, and made life miserable for those who remain. Today, students are being taught more about fringe academic subject mat-ter while core knowledge suffers. "Dumbing down" to accommodate poor preparation, limited English communication skills, and lowered expecta-tions have replaced true achievement. Mediocrity reins – but all nicely in compliance with governmental programs.

In a similar manner, 50 years ago, if one were sick or injured, a family physician was accessible – and would come to the patient if need be. Referral to a specialist or entry to more advanced hospital care was simple and the focus was on curing the patient, not ensuring payment to government agencies or insurance companies. If fact, over five decades, the entire focus of health care has shifted from medical care to medical payment. Layers of expensive bureaucracy have ensured that basic costs of care would be tripled or more to serve the paper mills of government and 3rd party payment systems.

When one walked into a doctor's office in earlier times there would be a receptionist, a nurse assistant, and a doctor or two. Today, for each of those professionals and support people, there are 3-4 more staff filling out forms. The poorest of patients could receive medical care under the "old" system, while those of modest means would pay proportionately, but not be wiped out financially by illness. Today, the only ones not at financial risk but with full access to health care are illegal immigrants, government employees, politicians, and incarcerated criminals.

Fifty years ago, family life was traditional, stable and predictable. The values of society encouraged family formation and continuity. Government was not the head of the family, nor the primary care giver, or financial steward – mothers and fathers were. As government took on more responsibilities "*in loco parentis*," the cost of government - and taxes - grew, placing still greater burdens on families. Since then "stay at home" moms have become a quaint anachronism; dads have become less responsible and accessible to their families; and children have been shuttled out to 24-hour care by one institution or another. Kids are screwed up in huge numbers, while drugs and dysfunction have become the norm – is it any wonder?

As if destruction of the family wasn't enough, we are now moving to make the concept of family irrelevant and to grant family standing to any two or more individuals who pledge their "love" in something ridiculously described as a "civil union." There is no need for motherhood, fatherhood, or childhood to have a family – *merely a village* of two or more. Once again, government has played a pivotal, and destructive, role.

Work used to define an individual – both in quality and quantity. There was a commitment to excellence which was rewarded by the loyalty of the employer. Whether large company or small, the formula was simple: fair and responsible ownership or management, dedicated and hard-working employees, and customers who were listened to and respected. Through a combination of taxation, unionization, and government regulation, all the participants have lost their bearings. Management has become greedy and paid obscene amounts of money without regard to true accomplishment; government approved mergers have led to dominance in industries while removing competitiveness and responsiveness to customers; loyalty among employers and employees has been rplaced by legal obligations – generally in response to government regulation. The work ethic has been replaced by victimhood or government handouts in one form or another.

Think about telecommunications, energy, and other areas of public utility. What is the one system that works almost flawlessly? *The Internet.* At present – though many are trying to change it – there is virtually no governmental involvement in the Internet. Is it surprising that it works so well? Telephone companies, energy suppliers, and the mail system used to be like that.

When Katrina hit this past year, another aspect of society was sacrificed: the local, charitable response to need. It is true, of course, that countless numbers of people gave incredible amounts of time, energy, and money in response to Katrina. But the reality is that it was all overshadowed by a huge involvement of government – huge sums of money, huge bureaucracy, huge amounts of regulation – and ultimately, huge failures as the private sector gave way to government. The great Chicago fire and the San Francisco earthquake were devastating to those cities – and yet there was no FEMA, nor was any president blamed for not responding fast enough or with enough federal bail-out money.

We still live in the best of all worlds - the best of all countries. But if we go forward into 2006 with one goal, that goal should be clear: To return our institutions to greatness by lessening or removing the stranglehold of government that has so diminished them in the first place. Government, especially the federal government, is not the solution – it is, as Ronald Reagan pointed out, the problem. The less we have of it, the better our chances of returning to greatness will improve. It's a new year – let's get started.

§

THE PAPER ROUTE
Lessons in Growing Up *(NOV 2003)*

"I'm a great believer in luck, and I find the harder I work the more I have of it."
       ~ *Thomas Jefferson*

A great hallmark in growing up has been lost in the past generation or two: *the paper route*. It used to be a rite of passage from childhood to adolescence. At about age 10 or so, a young boy (or girl) would go on down to the local weekly paper and apply for the coveted job. Mom or dad might go with you, but just as often as not you were encouraged to ride your bike down, walk on in, and just do it yourself. That was the first lesson of the process – *choice*. Beyond that seemingly simple but wonderful discovery there was a glimmer of self-esteem germinating inside of you. You had actually taken the initiative to do something, and God willing, and your bicycle staying serviceable, you were going to do it.

Then you got the job. They didn't guarantee the route was going to be in your neighborhood and in fact it might be several neighborhoods removed, but still "bikeable." Then they explained the rules. You were not just a paperboy – you were a businessman. They delivered the papers to you and billed you for them. It was up to you to count them and make sure you weren't "shorted." On top of that, while they would help you by selling subscriptions, you had to collect each month from your customers – cash, check or money order. Often the process required several trips. Occasionally, someone skipped or refused to pay, but those instances were rare, even though at your expense. You took the responsibility and assumed the risks.

The job wasn't easy – especially if you had a morning route. Of course, either way you had to make choices. A morning route meant getting up early – before school – getting your papers, folding, banding, bagging (technical jargon for the trade), and delivering. Then coming back to get ready for school. Homework better have already been done. Of course, if you had the afternoon route, you had more flexibility, but your afternoon playtime became cramped. If guys wanted to go down to the creek, you had to pass – *you* had papers to deliver. You had responsibilities. You made choices and had a duty to honor them.

Rain or shine the papers had to go out. If there was a chance of rain, there was the added task of putting papers into wrappers to protect them; more work, no more pay. Life was unfair that way, but you dealt with it. If it was raining hard, mom might take pity and drive you down to get the papers so you could fold them at home, and even take you on the route in the car if the weather was really bad. Of course, if it wasn't, the yellow raincoat came out.

There were two kinds of bags to carry papers. One type fit over your bike's fender like a saddlebag, thought there was also a smaller capacity, front basket model. The other type fit over your head and shoulders with papers front and rear. I don't think OSHA would have approved, and there weren't any trial lawyers lurking about in case you took a spill. You invariably did. If so, you looked around to make sure that no one saw you.

It was hard but satisfying work. The money was pretty good and, after all, there weren't a lot of options for a 10-year-old. The lessons were great, but no one went into the newspaper delivery "business" for lessons at that age. It would be years before the value of it all sank in. In my case, about 46 of them.

If you stuck with it, in a couple of years you might have the credentials to move on to the big time: *the daily paper*. Now that was work. A route might include 200-250 customers. That's a lot of papers to pick up, fold, band, and bag. But then, a couple of hundred customers, 7 days a week… now that was a lot of moola! More than one kid paid for the necessities of his young life, and a few paid their way through college on that kind of money. Hard earned, self-respected, and self-collected money.

Of course, if you lived in the typical household, when you started making a little money a strange thing happened. You were expected to shoulder a little of the family burden. Some of the little things that had always been footed by mom or the old man suddenly became your capability – *and responsibility.* There's that word again. You whined a little at first – but you settled into it as being a not so unreasonable thing. After a while, it actually became a source of pride (I believe that is where self-esteem comes from). Then something else happened. You became a little more value conscious. It was your money. You worked hard for it. You were a little more careful about how you spent it. Bargains and sales were something to be sought out.

Well, kids don't have paper routes anymore. And that's a damn shame. There are great lessons of life that have been lost on kids because of that – and playing video games is not going to fill the void. I have a fond memory of those lessons and a pride in the effort that was required to learn them. Kids today lead more sheltered lives, protected from responsibility, initiative, and hard work. It's little wonder that so many still live at home as adults; more victims from the loss of reason, justice, and common sense.

§

EPILOGUE
AMERICA
What's So Great About It?

"The greatness of America lies not in being more enlightened than any other nation, but rather in her ability to repair her faults."
  ~ *Alexis de Tocqueville*

AMERICA
What's So Great About it? *(JUL 2004)*

They hate us – or so we hear. From Europe to Mexico; from Canada to Africa – the world is at odds with the United States. "Who appointed us the world's policeman?" "How can we justify the consumption of more resources than other nations?" "Who are we to impose our democratic, capitalist way of life on others?" Of course, the major media and much of our educational establishment echoes these "hate America" slogans (while they prosper under its umbrella of blessings).

Ask any of these critics, though, "If not America, then who?" Ask them "What kind of world would it be if not for the United States of America?" The answer is likely to be a stuttered and feeble explanation or an embarrassed silence.

In fact, the United States is by broad measure the greatest country on earth, and likely in the history of civilization. By accomplishment alone, such a proclamation would be hard to deny. But it's in the essence of its guiding principles, its character, and its leadership that our country has risen to this noble place in history.

The founding principles of this nation are a distillation of the great thoughts on liberty from the Greeks and Romans through the English empire from which we sought and achieved our emancipation. Jefferson and his fellow patriots found the ultimate simplicity in defining our basis for existence as "self evident" and "endowed by our Creator."

While our freedom is threatened both from within and without, we are still the most free nation on earth. Our system of justice and equality, while imperfect, is the most universally embraced and promulgated in the world. Our spirit of independence has been weakened by decades of increased dependence on well-intending government programs, though we are still prepared to fight to maintain it. America still offers the world's greatest forum in which to seek and pursue our personal happiness and to realize our dreams, no matter how simple or lofty. Too often, we have lost sight of the duties which accompany this great opportunity. As thousands of young people still volunteer and serve in our armed forces, we know in our hearts the cost of preserving liberty.

The presence of government in our lives has grown leviathan-like, but unlike may other governments, it is still limited by the constitutional restraints we have at our disposal if the balance tips too far. Our government is still, in fact, a government "of the people, by the people, and for the people." If it becomes abusive or unresponsive as perceived by the people, a mark on a ballot, a citizen initiative, or a popular recall can place it in check. Should it become destructive to the ends for which it was formed, still greater power is enshrined "to alter, or abolish it."

If the structure of our country is a marvel to the world, the character of its inhabitants is even more so.

Americans are among the most giving and compassionate on earth. When disaster strikes anywhere in the world, there is an outpouring of love, concern – and most visibly obvious – action, that speaks volumes for the kind of people we are. Whether those in trouble are friends or strangers, allies or enemies, it requires only a "need" to rally the response of the Americans to come to their aid. Tragedy in the world is never met with indifference, and the response from this country is at all levels. Even in times of war, we have responded to attack by our enemies by defeating them – and then assisting in the rebuilding their broken nations. The response can be no less for a nation born of Christian traditions – and it is not.

An American birthright is optimism. From the daunting challenge of the fight to secure our first freedoms from England, we have always seen fit to challenge adversity. If the glass is half empty, we'll fill it. If the battle is above our ability, we'll rise to it. If the need is greater than our capacity, we'll meet it. Whether soaring to the unknown risks of heavenly exploration, or facing the inevitable challenges on earth, Americans have the courage, tenacity, and inventiveness to shrink from nothing that limits them.

To a visitor from Mars, the picture painted by our television and other entertainment venues would be one of moral decay, depravity, and self-indulgence to an extreme. A closer examination, however, would reveal a nation of people much more committed to virtue than those public vignettes suggest. We are still a nation of Godly principles and of virtuous intentions. We are very aware of our human limits and the challenges of achieving good in our thoughts and deeds. The battle of preserving personal choice, while offering public example, is challenging and the pendulum invariably swings back to a more virtuous balance over time.

Our "melting pot" texture has sadly become more a pot of mixed vegetables with separate needs and wants, rather than a collective culture reflecting the best of all its elements. Still, we are tolerant and considerate of needs arising from differences. To a fault sometimes, we accommodate such differences, and the costs are burdensome. As a result, we are often challenged, sometimes divided; but we remain the most tolerant people in the world. The very nature of our freedom compels us to be.

The leadership of the world is in the hands of the Americans. It has not happened by choice, but by natural progression based on the truths embodied in our founding principles. Our political foundations are the model for all the world that is free, or yearns to be. Every emerging country, if the truth were told, would strive for a Constitution and a system of opportunity and justice much like ours. The system of reward by achievement has given rise to inventiveness and economic success that is the envy of the world.

Therein lies the basis for much of the so-called "hatred" for America. It is not just our own lives that are enriched by such tangible achievement; the lives of people around the world have been enhanced because of advances, inventions, and trade made possible by the wealth of America. The world has adopted English as a universal language for a reason – and that reason is the leadership of America in science, technology, and commerce.

As suggested, our moral principles are not always the purest or the most "correct." Still, they offer the world's best hope for fair and equitable treatment of its citizens. Despite its limitations and its failures, the moral leadership of the United States is still, objectively, the fairest standard available to mankind. Would we substitute that of the Middle East, where a woman might be stoned to death for adultery? Or that of some nations where mere dissent is grounds for murder? Our moral code is far from perfect, in either its design or its implementation, but it is the best there is.

If the French or Germans or Canadians were to be attacked, where would they look for military support? Russia? China? Poland? Libya? The answer is painfully clear. The mere presence or proximity of American military in or to foreign nations has given comfort to them in very real terms. As such, other nations spend a fraction for defense as compared to the U.S. – they don't have to pay for it, because we provide it. There is security in possessing the most powerful military might in the history of the world. There is also great duty in using it to help ensure world peace. America has met its duty time after time, and continues to do so – even when mocked by those who lead lives in peace as a result of it.

The real appreciation of American military might will only be understood by others when we remove its protective presence from their shores. It is time to do so – though we will, as we always have, be prepared to lend our might to defend freedom and justice anywhere it is needed. No other nation on earth can, has, or will exercise that prerogative.

If we have a weakness in ourselves, it is a failure to accept the greatness of our nation and the example it sets for the rest of the world. You see, they don't hate us. They sometimes envy us; they often emulate us; and they always depend on us for their comfort and protection. They wish and strive for what we have achieved, and we are generous in sharing.

We must remain confident, not arrogant; we must be humble in our good fortune. We must never, though, fail to recognize the incredible greatness of our nation, nor the means and sacrifice by which that greatness was achieved. God bless America.

§

MEA CULPA

"I cling to my imperfection, as the very essence of my being."
     ~ Anatole France

In writing essays about the way the world is or ought to be, some might think the author of such thoughts to be of exemplery stature. I am not. Though I have written of the importance of stable families, I confess to my own shortcomings as a divorced man. Though I have written on the importance of God and moral behavior, I confess to my own sins and shortcomings, both numerous and varied. Though I have written critically of those in elective office, I have chosen not to pursue such endeavors myself, believing my contribution is better made in the writing, rather than in the doing.

In short, my imperfections are many, but my love of God, country, family, and community cannot be challenged. Nor can my belief in the most fundamental rights granted to us by our Creator: "Life, liberty, and the pursuit of happiness." Those sacred rights are under attack as never before and no amount of human imperfection can lessen the duty each of us has to restore them.

I am completely guilty of that offense; I encourage others to join me.

"I would remind you that extremism in the defense of liberty is no vice! And let me remind you also that moderation in the pursuit of justice is no virtue."
     ~ Barry Goldwater

§